a **WEE GUIDE** *to*
Mary, Queen of Scots

a **WEE GUIDE** *to*

Mary, Queen of Scots

Joyce Miller

GOBLINSHEAD

Edinburgh

a *Wee Guide* to Mary, Queen of Scots

First Published 1996
Reprinted 1997, 1999, 2001
© Martin Coventry 1996
Text © Joyce Miller, Martin Coventry
Published by **GOBLINSHEAD**
130B Inveresk Road
Musselburgh EH21 7AY
Scotland
tel 0131 665 2894; *fax* 0131 653 6566
email goblinshead@sol.co.uk

British Library Cataloguing in Publication Data
A catalogue record for this book is available from the British Library.

ISBN 1 899874 03 8

Typeset by **GOBLINSHEAD** using Desktop Publishing
Typeset in Garamond Narrow

Wee Guides
- **Scottish History**
- **Prehistoric Scotland** • **The Picts**
- **Macbeth and Early Scotland**
- **St Margaret and Malcolm Canmore**
- **William Wallace** • **Robert the Bruce**
- **Mary, Queen of Scots**
- **The Jacobites** • **Rob Roy MacGregor** • **Flora MacDonald**
- **Robert Burns** • **Whisky**
- **Haunted Castles of Scotland** • **Scottish Ghosts and Bogles**

Look Out for Goblinshead's Thistle Guide series

a **WEE GUIDE** *to*
Mary, Queen of Scots

Contents

List of maps

List of illustrations

Acknowledgements

The illustrations on the following pages are reproduced by kind permission: The Execution of Mary, Queen of Scots, by Robert Herdman (front cover, detail, and page 68) Glasgow Art Gallery and Museum, Kelvingrove; James V and Mary of Guise by an unknown artist (page 7) from the collection at Blair Castle, Perthshire; Mary, Queen of Scots by François Clouet (page 23) Photographie Bibliothèque Nationale, Paris; Murder of David Rizzio by Sir William Allan (page 49) The National Gallery of Scotland, Edinburgh; Mary, Queen of Scots, and Darnley at Jedburgh by Alfred Elmore (page 52) reproduced by courtesy of Astley House - Fine Art of Moreton-in-Marsh, Gloucestershire; Earl of Bothwell by an unknown artist (page 56) The Scottish National Portrait Gallery, Edinburgh; photograph of Traquair House (page 84) by Anna Coventry; photograph of Neidpath Castle (page 82) by Janine Hunter. Other photographs by Martin Coventry, except Etal Castle (page 5), Renaissance fountain, Linlithgow Palace (page 9), Louvre Palace (page 19), Edzell Castle (page 32), and Jedburgh Abbey (page 80) by Joyce Miller.

Many thanks to everyone who has contributed to the completion of this small book, including Dr Helen Dingwall, Dilys Jones, Barbara Mahon, Ruby and Tom Miller, Aileen Turnbull, and my publisher Martin Coventry.

How to use this book

This book is divided into two sections:

- The text (pages 2–71) describes Mary's life and the events surrounding her, with five maps (pages 4, 14, 36, 40 & 46). A family tree illustrates the relationship of Mary to the monarchs of Scotland, England and France (page 42).

- Places, associated with Mary, to visit (pages 72–86) listing over 50 castles and abbeys. Information includes access, opening days, facilities, and a brief description; and a map locates all the sites (page 70).

An index (pages 87–88) lists all the main people, battles and events.

Warning

While the information in this book was believed to be correct at time of going to press – and was checked, where possible, with the visitor attractions – opening times and facilities, or other information, may vary or differ from that included. All information should be checked with the visitor attractions before embarking on any journey. Inclusion in the text is no indication whatsoever that a site is open to the public or that it should be visited. Many sites, particularly ruined castles, are potentially dangerous and great care should be taken: the publisher and author cannot accept responsibility for damage or injury caused from any visit.

The places listed to visit are only a personal selection of what is available in Scotland, and the inclusion or exclusion of a visitor attraction in the text should not be considered as a comment or judgement on that attraction.

Locations on maps may be approximate.

Introduction

Growing up, and being educated in Scotland, left me for much of my life with a sorely inadequate knowledge of Scottish history. However one reign and its outcome did manage to become lodged in my general mythology of the Scottish nation – that of Mary, who ended her life imprisoned and had her head chopped off by Elizabeth of England. Another observation, of no great consequence, was that Mary appeared to have stayed in almost every building of note throughout lowland Scotland.

It was these basic observations that were the inspirations for this book – to learn more about Mary herself, and to compile a guide to places of interest which were associated with her. The narrative of Mary's life should be read neither to excuse nor accuse her of failing as a monarch, but to describe the events and problems that she faced and to present her human side. The guide to places, along with the maps, provides information about visiting and access for those who enjoy the visual pleasure of history, as much as reading about it.

JM, Edinburgh, November 1996

Calendar of events

1513   Scots lose battle of Flodden against English. James IV slain.

1542   Scots defeated by English at the Battle of Solway Moss. Birth of Mary. Death of James V.

1543   Peace treaty between Scots and English: Mary to marry Edward, Henry VIII's son. Mary crowned at Stirling, but Scots renege on betrothal.

1544-5 *Rough Wooing*: south-eastern Scotland ravaged by English.

1546   Cardinal Beaton murdered. St Andrews castle besieged.

1547   Scots crushed at the Battle of Pinkie by English. English invade south-east Scotland.

1548   Mary sent to France. Marriage contract between Mary and Dauphin, François, agreed. Scotland ruled by the Earl of Arran and Mary of Guise.

1550   English pushed out of Scotland with French help.

1557   *First Bond* signed by Protestant lords.

1558   Mary and François married. Start of religious unrest in Scotland.

1559   François becomes King of France. Mary of Guise Regent.

1560   Death of Mary of Guise. Peace agreed between Scots, English and French. François dies.

1561   Mary returns to Scotland.

1562   Mary's forces defeat the Earl of Huntly's troops at the Battle of Corrichie.

1563   French poet Châtelard forces his way into Mary's bedchamber, and is executed.

1565   Mary and Darnley meet and, despite opposition by some nobles, marry at Holyrood. *Chaseabout Raid*: those opposed to Darnley rebel, but are hounded out of Scotland. Mary supported by Bothwell.

1566   Rizzio, Mary's favourite, murdered. Darnley involved in plot. James VI born at Edinburgh Castle. Mary visits injured Bothwell at Hermitage Castle. James VI baptized at Stirling. Mary and Darnley attempt reconciliation.

1567   Darnley murdered at Kirk o' Field, Edinburgh, and the house blown up. Suspicion falls on Mary, but Bothwell accused, although officially acquitted. Bothwell kidnaps Mary in April, and they marry in May. *Confederate Lords* march to Borthwick Castle, where Mary and Bothwell are staying. They escape but

Mary's forces are defeated at Carberry Hill in June. Mary imprisoned in Lochleven castle, where she agrees to abdicate. Bothwell escapes to the continent, but is imprisoned at Dragsholm in Denmark. James VI crowned.

1568   Mary escapes from Lochleven and flees to the west. Hamiltons and others raise army for her, but her forces are crushed at the Battle of Langside. Mary flees to England and asks for Elizabeth's help. Elizabeth imprisons Mary, and Mary spends the next 19 years in captivity in England.

1570   Regent Moray murdered.

1571   Regent Lennox shot and killed at Stirling. *Ridolfi Plot*: Mary plots against Elizabeth with Duke of Norfolk, who is executed.

1572   Regent Mar dies.

1573   End of civil war in Scotland. Mary's party crushed.

1578   Death of Bothwell at Dragsholm.

1581   Morton, Regent from 1572-8, is executed.

1585   James VI begins to assert control of Scotland.

1586   *Babington Plot*: to assassinate Elizabeth and put Mary on throne. Those involved in plot tried and executed. Mary moved to Fotheringhay Castle to stand trial for her part in plot, and is found guilty.

1587   Mary executed.

1603   Union of Crowns of Scots and England: James ascends to the English throne.

Map 1: 1513–48 (Chapters 1–2)

1 – Stewart Scotland

Mary, Queen of Scots was executed at Fotheringhay Castle, in England, in 1587. Some have seen her as a martyr, others as a failure. She inherited the Scottish crown when she was only six days old, during a period of strife in Scotland, and indeed the rest of Europe. She then spent 13 years in France from the age of five, and later 19 years in captivity in England. During these years Mary spent a mere seven years in Scotland, when she ruled the country in her own right. Whatever opinion is about Mary's personal rule, she faced many unique problems during her reign, not the least being the religious changes which occurred during the Reformation. She has often been compared unfavourably to other Stewart monarchs – perhaps because they were male – and yet neither her father nor grandfather might be seen as having been any more successful.

In 1542, the year of Mary's birth, James V – her father – followed *his* more popular father's example by commanding a Scottish army to yet another major defeat by the English. The battle at Solway Moss may not have resulted in such a huge loss of life as Flodden, but the consequences of the battle were just as serious for the kingdom and the Scots.

Because of a mutual defence agreement made with France, James IV had led his army of men, drawn from throughout his kingdom, highland and lowland, to battle at Flodden in 1513 against the old enemy England. Both Louis XII of France and James were aware that Henry VIII of England might plan to invade either, or both, their kingdoms. Henry VIII's invasion of France led to James's invasion of Northumberland, while Henry was occupied in France. But Henry had left contingency plans anticipating this

Etal Castle – an exhibition here tells the story of Flodden

possibility, and had left the Earl of Surrey with the power to assemble an army if required. Surrey was able to call up 26 000 men, as against James's 35 000, and challenged the Scots to battle on 9 September 1513. The odds may have been with James theoretically, but the tactical superiority of the English, and the use of short bills (a short spear-like weapon which could be used either to stab like a spear or slash like an axe) which proved more effective than the Scottish pikes (fifteen-foot long spears which required skill and training to use effectively, neither of which the Scots had), contributed to a heavy loss of life. There may have been as many as 9 000 Scots slain, and 4 000 English, but most seriously for the Scots was the loss of their popular king, and many of his most senior nobles and advisors.

When James V succeeded to the throne at the tender age of 17 months Scotland again had a minor as a monarch and government by regency. The rivalries between some of the oldest families in Scotland did little to restore peace to a country which had suffered the loss of so many men. The mutual defence alliance continued with France, and therefore relations with England remained distinctly distant, despite the fact that the Queen Mother was Margaret Tudor, Henry VIII's sister.

James V was very much the opposite of his father. James IV had been an energetic and popular king. He was intelligent, tall and athletic, spoke several languages including Gaelic, and was a true renaissance king interested in music, art, architecture and science. He remodelled the royal palaces of Linlithgow, Falkland and Holyrood Palace, Edinburgh; attempted to establish a Scottish navy by building the *Great Michael* and founded a new university at Aberdeen. He also ratified the establishment of an Incorporation of Surgeons in Edinburgh in 1506 as a result of his interest in science and medicine. His son had few of these accomplishments apart from continuing the Stewart male's success with women, producing several illegitimate children.

In 1528 when James V was 16 years old, he took over ruling the kingdom in his own right, and attempted to crush the Douglases who had imprisoned him during his minority. He also attempted to restore law and order in outlying areas of the country, particularly the borders, highlands and islands. Unfortunately although his heavy-handedness may have restored a form of order it did little to inspire loyalty and confidence in the king. Having alienated the Douglases, he then went on to alienate the Armstrongs in the borders and the MacDonalds in the highlands. The removal from power of these major families led to others becoming equally dominant, and in later years they would not come to James's support when he was at war with

England. James also abused his monarch's right of appointments to the major church benefices by granting five of his illegitimate sons rich positions. By placing them in positions of authority in the church, he ensured that the church supported royal authority and was a major source of income for the crown.

During James's reign international events affected Scotland's domestic situation as much as her relations with other countries. One of the major European developments, which was to influence Scotland over the next generation, was the start of the religious Reformation in Europe. Also important were the relations, cordial or otherwise, between the major powers of England, France, Spain and the Holy Roman Empire in which Scotland had its part to play.

Royal marriages were always important and often did not involve love or even attraction. Dynastic associations and allegiances between countries were at the forefront of most marriage negotiations. James's choice of bride was of international importance despite the fact that Scotland was not as powerful as France or England. Neither France nor England wished James to marry a Spanish bride, but a French bride was also an unacceptable choice to the English.

The nominal peace which had been established between England and Scotland continued, but there were repeated minor skirmishes involving the two countries. By 1533 France would not support Scotland against England as relations were relatively friendly between the two. Henry VIII, because of

James V and Mary of Guise: portrait by an unknown artist

7

his religious stance, was isolated from the rest of Europe and looked to his northern relative to support him, but as James had burnt Protestant heretics in the 1530s, he had no intention of breaking with Rome, and the rest of Europe, on Henry's behalf.

By 1536 James had made clear his intention of marrying a French bride and a marriage to Princess Madeleine of France was arranged. She died less than six months after their wedding, but James found another suitable bride in Mary of Guise, and thus managed to acquire two large French dowries in the process. This bound Scotland and France even more tightly. Charles V, the Holy Roman Emperor, and François I of France signed treaties in 1537 and 1538, supporting the actions of the Pope against Henry, but this allegiance of old rivals did not last and by 1541 both independently asked Henry for his support against the other.

In Scotland, James's avarice and his heavy-handed government contributed to a dwindling loyalty amongst his subjects, and to some extent the growth of a pro-English party among some Scots, which was to have serious consequences.

The final crisis of 1542 was the culmination of personal loss, domestic mismanagement and international events. In the spring of 1541 the two young sons of James and Mary of Guise both died, a loss of the security of succession so vital to reigning monarchs. The following year Henry, who still hoped to persuade his nephew to join with him, asked him to a meeting at York. James agreed to attend but his privy council were against the proposal, both out of fear for James's life and because the Scottish clergy were against Henry's religious policy and did not want James to follow his example. Henry VIII, in retaliation for the non-appearance of James, organized his forces for an invasion of Scotland. Sir Robert Bowes, who headed Henry's army, was aided by the exiled Earl of Angus and others of the Douglas family. However despite initial successes by the English, Scottish troops led by the Earl of Huntly, George Gordon, and the Earl of Home, ambushed a party of Englishmen and chased them back to their main camp at Haddon Rigg. At the consequent battle the Scots were victorious, and took about 600 prisoners, killing another 400 including Bowes himself. Henry's response was to send north an even greater number of men. The Scots failed to capitalize on their advantages, and lack of provisions contributed to a discontented army. James, instead of working with the victorious Huntly, blamed him for 'inaction' and replaced him with the Earl of Moray, as a result alienating yet more of his nobles.

France and England were at this time in a period of feud, and due to his loyalty and obligations to his old ally, and perhaps hoping to avenge the disaster at Flodden, James felt honour-bound to organize a major attack on England. He was quickly to discover that the size of force that he was able to summon was very much less than that of his father. The numbers have been put at between 14 000 and 20 000.

James left Edinburgh, leaving Moray with some troops at Haddington and proceeded to Lochmaben near Dumfries with the rest of his army. He intended to march across the Solway sands and meet up with more Scottish troops, led by Oliver Sinclair, who was not a noble but was one of James's favourites. Sinclair's troops were attacked at Solway Moss on the 14 November 1542. In the event,

relatively few Scots were killed, but 1200 were taken prisoner and it was not to James's credit that so many of his troops were unwilling to die for their king.

After his defeat, James headed back via Peebles to Edinburgh, spent a week at Linlithgow with his queen, who was in the late stages of pregnancy, then left for Falkland Palace. It was there he took to his bed, a broken, disappointed man, whose last hours have provided the history books with as much to say as the whole of his previous thirty years. As he lay on his death bed, he awaited news of his wife's delivery,

Renaissance fountain – Linlithgow Palace

perhaps hoping that a male child would at least ensure the Stewart succession.

In December Mary of Guise was delivered of a girl, the news of which provided one of the most frequently quoted sayings of Scottish history – *it cam wi a lass and it'll gang wi a lass.* With the death of her father on 14 December, Scotland had lost one of its least popular Stewart monarchs and was left with a six-day old queen. The life of James's daughter would prove to be even more complicated and eventful than that of her father.

2 – The infant Queen

On the 8 December 1542 a baby girl was born at Linlithgow Palace. Although her father knew of her birth he would never see her, as he died when she was just six days old. The infant Mary became queen of Scots at this tender age, and as a result of her father's precipitous death, the consequences of religious strife and political struggles in Scotland as well as in the rest of Europe, the life of this child-queen was never going to be straightforward.

Following the death of James, the war with Henry VIII and England was ended after negotiations conducted by James Hamilton, Earl of Arran, who, as the heir presumptive, had been appointed Lord Governor to rule Scotland during Mary's minority. The treaties that Arran agreed to at Greenwich in July 1543 included terms for peace and for the marriage of Mary to Henry VIII's son Edward, but they were not popular with many of

Stirling Castle

the Scots nobles. The infant Queen was taken to Stirling Castle by her mother for safety, where she was crowned in the Chapel Royal on 9 September. As Mary was an infant, she had nothing to do with the running of the country, and The Governor (Arran), her mother and Cardinal Beaton administered the country on her behalf. Apart from uneasy relations with England, the Scottish regency had both internal political and religious problems, and relations with France to deal with. Political loyalties were influenced to some extent by religious beliefs or persuasion, and the triumvirate was not always united. Mary of Guise and Catholic Cardinal Beaton were essentially pro-French, but Arran, along with some of the other Scottish nobles including Cassillis, Angus, Glencairn and Rothes, were more pro-English in both political and religious matters.

By December 1543 the Scottish parliament had repudiated the Treaties of Greenwich, much to Henry's annoyance. When Arran had agreed to them, the political allegiances of the Scots were complicated by their religious affiliation, and the eventual rejection of the treaties led to a revival of Catholic power in Scotland, led by Cardinal Beaton and Mary of Guise. Their supporters included Huntly, Lennox, Argyll and Bothwell. Although Beaton's policy was ostensibly religious in nature, his attempts to stamp out the spread of heresy and anti-Catholic feeling in the country, resulted in severe political and economic consequences. In retaliation for the behaviour of the Scots Henry embarked on a series of raids into Scotland during 1544 and 1545, mainly in the border area, but also as far north as Edinburgh. These raids, known as the *Rough Wooing,* were led by the Earl of Hertford, and resulted in the looting and burning of the abbeys at Holyrood Palace, Melrose, Jedburgh, Kelso and Dryburgh. Crops and ships were also stolen.

Not all of the Scottish nobles suffered badly from these events, as some duplicitous families, (the *Assured Scots*) such as the Grays, swore allegiance to Henry as a result of bribery or bullying, and were granted pensions. During the early years of the *Rough Wooing*, the Scots were not very successful in dealing with the English, but the tables were turned at Ancrum Moor (near Jedburgh) early in 1545. As a result of the destruction of the Douglas Tomb at Melrose by a troop of English, Scots and mercenaries, the Earl of Angus (a Douglas himself and until then a supporter of the English) along with Scott of Buccleuch and Lesley of Rothes led about 1500 men against 3000 English troops under Sir Ralph Eure. Although the resulting defeat and slaughter of the English temporarily raised the morale of the Scots, it did not end the war.

At the time of the *Rough Wooing* other events were taking place in Scotland which would have long-term effects on the country. Throughout the sixteenth century, the Reformation affected the whole of Europe, and Scotland was no exception. In the eastern ports of Aberdeen, Dundee, Leith and St Andrews Lutheran ideas and literature were imported. Much has been written about whether the Scottish Reformation was a result of dissatisfaction with the Catholic church, which was accused of corruption and greed, or an increasing desire for the individual spirituality and responsibility advocated by protestantism. Whatever the reasons, during the 1540s and 1550s there was as much religious as political unrest in Scotland. Cardinal Beaton, as Archbishop of St Andrews, was head of the church in Scotland. He also had great political power as he was appointed Chancellor in January 1543 and as such influenced the policies of the first administration during Mary's minority. The practice of celibacy by clerics was not officially sanctioned by the church until the final debates of the Council of Trent in 1564 and so, like many other churchmen of the time, Cardinal Beaton had a mistress by whom he had three children. Beaton built Melgund Castle (near Brechin) for them.

Although he may not have burnt as many heretics as in other countries, Beaton still sent several to the stake, most importantly George Wishart. The burning of Wishart at St Andrews in 1546 may have been a turning point for the Reformation in Scotland, and it was certainly to prove very serious for Beaton himself. As a result of this execution, Norman Leslie, James Melville, Kirkcaldy of Grange and some others stole into St Andrews Castle where Beaton was, and murdered him. His naked dead body was hung from one of the windows to demonstrate what had been done in retaliation for Wishart's death.

The removal of Beaton from the political and religious scene did not lead to an overall *volte face*, or reversal, in Scottish politics and religion. Mary of Guise's own personal authority increased and, as a result of her influence, Arran ordered the castle to be besieged. The siege of St Andrews Castle might have resulted in a humiliating defeat for Mary and Arran as the castle was well provided with food and ammunition to withstand an attack of several months. Among the besieged was John Knox, who would court controversy on several occasions in the future.

The stalemate was not broken, even by the English reinforcing the castle, until the French appeared in support of Mary. The French king François I had died and his successor Henri II had placed the Duke of Guise and the Cardinal of Lorraine, Mary of Guise's brothers, in positions of power. They sent a fleet of 20 ships whose ordnance was to prove successful against the English troops and the Castilians. The mine and counter-mine which were tunnelled under St Andrews Castle during the siege can still be seen.

During the first few years of her life, Mary was brought up with her half-brothers and sisters, Lord James, Lord Robert and Lady Jean Stewart speaking Scots, well away from the day-to-day problems of the country. As well as assuring her future as queen, her mother had Mary's immediate future survival to consider, as the threat from England persisted.

With the death of Henry in January 1547, the English crown also passed to a minor, Edward VI, but the country was governed by the Earl of Hertford, now the Duke of Somerset, who built forts in the south-east of Scotland from Berwick to Dundee, concentrating his English troops at Haddington. He engaged the Scots in battle at Pinkie, near Musselburgh, on 9 September

1547. The Scots were led by the Earl of Arran and there were reportedly 30 000 men drawn from throughout Scotland. Unfortunately, although the Scots outnumbered the English, the English were more professionally organized, trained and equipped, and by the end of the fighting 10 000 Scots were dead and a further 1500 taken prisoner. Pinkie was a victory for the English, but hostilities between the two countries were to continue for another three years, and increased Scottish dependency on France.

Mary's safety was paramount and the threat of possible capture by English troops led to her being moved around the country: in 1547 she was sent to Inchmahome Priory (on the Lake of Mentieth, near Stirling) but by

Inchmahome Priory

1548 she had been moved to Dumbarton Castle. In 1548 English troops burnt Dunbar Castle; Musselburgh, near Edinburgh; and Dalkeith – and fortified Haddington.

French troops returned to Scotland to help the Scots besiege Haddington, but in return Henri II offered to provide Mary a safe haven along with eventual marriage to his son François, the Dauphin. The French landed at Leith and with the Scots marched on Haddington. By 7 July 1548 the Treaty of Haddington between the Scots and the French was signed at the Nunnery of Haddington and at the age of four years and seven months, Mary was betrothed for the second time.

Map 2: 1548–63 (Chapters 3–6)

3 – Childhood in France

With the signing of the Treaty of Haddington, Mary was placed in even greater danger of being taken prisoner by the English, and at King Henri's suggestion, plans were made to send her to France. By July 1548, Mary was at Dumbarton Castle, and the French fleet sailed round the north coast of Scotland, came up the Clyde estuary and picked Mary up from Dumbarton. Several others embarked with Mary. The Lords Erskine and Livingston were sent as her guardians, Jean Sinclair as her nurse, and Lady Fleming as her governess. As companions she had three of her half brothers, illegitimate sons of James V, as well as other sons and daughters of the Scottish nobility, including in particular the four Marys – Fleming, Livingston, Seton and Beaton. Mary Fleming was related to the Royal House of Stewart through her mother. Mary Beaton was of the family of the murdered Cardinal Beaton. Mary Seton's father was Lord Seton, who was to remain loyal to Mary throughout her life, and Mary Livingston was the daughter of Lord Livingston. Because of their noble birth they were acceptable as ladies-in-waiting for the Queen. The fleet set sail on the 7 August 1548 and arrived near Roscoff (Brittany) on the coast of France six days later.

The next 13 years may have been the happiest and most carefree for Mary. Under the protection of her French grandparents Claud and Antoinette, Duke and Duchess of Guise, her half-brother François Duke of Longueville from her mother's first marriage, and many other uncles and aunts of the powerful Guise-Lorraine family she could, perhaps for the first time, freely enjoy the splendour and pleasures of courtly life.

The Guise court may not have been royal, but to all intents and purposes the power and influence emanating from this extended dynasty was in many ways equal to Henri's. It was here that Mary started her proper education; having been brought up speaking Scots she now had to learn French, and eventually mastered Latin, Italian, Spanish and Greek. She actively participated in music and dancing – playing the lute and writing poetry, something she was to continue doing throughout her adult life. Mary also became an accomplished horsewoman and enjoyed riding and hunting. As her French relatives were Catholic, there was no doubt that Mary would be brought up in the Catholic faith. Although she remained a Catholic until her death, it would add to her problems when she returned to Scotland in 1561, as by then this form of worship had been forbidden by the Scottish parliament.

At this time, an early return to Scotland was not included in the plans of

Mary's Guise relatives or indeed Henri himself. Although Mary was the crowned monarch of Scotland, it was the role of queen of France for which she was now being groomed. It was at the Castle of Carrières (Chateau de Carrières) near St Germain that Mary met her betrothed for the first time. Despite his physical failings – he was unhealthy and fragile – Mary and François liked each other.

Henri was also pleased with his future daughter-in-law and welcomed her into the royal court, where she spent much time with other young royals. Henri gradually reduced the influence of Mary's Scottish advisors and friends by separating her from them more and more. The French royal court, like others of the time, was peripatetic and moved from one castle to another enjoying the culture of the court and the produce of the land. The future looked bright for Mary and François, and although she corresponded frequently with her beloved mother, the problems Mary of Guise faced as Regent of Scotland did not hold much interest for a young girl. Training in political skills was not part of Mary's education at this time, but in later years she would find that diplomacy would be an important feature of royal rule and administration.

During the years that Mary spent in France, the war between England and Scotland continued, and despite the French presence final defeat of the English proved to be an elusive goal. It was not until troubles in England forced the Duke of Somerset, known as Protector Somerset, to return home, followed by the rest of the English troops chased out by a combination of the arrival of further French troops, famine and disease, that peace was agreed. Peace between France and England was negotiated at the Treaty of Boulogne in March 1550, and finally peace between Scotland and England in June 1551. Following the removal of English troops from Scotland, Mary of Guise had then to be careful that the presence of large numbers of French did not alienate the Scottish nobles. Many of the French were sent home, but those that remained held important positions in the queen mother's household. After the signing of the treaty at Boulogne, Mary of Guise visited France in order to request more French support to suppress the progress of the Reformation in Scotland and to support her claim to replace Arran as regent.

James Hamilton, second Earl of Arran, was head of one of the most powerful families in Scotland, and although by inclination Protestant, his loyalty wavered. His agenda was at times pro-English or pro-Protestant, occasionally the two coinciding, but mainly it was to ensure the advancement of the Hamilton power base and to strengthen the family's claim to the throne. Arran, along with Matthew Stewart, Earl of Lennox, could claim a direct line back to James II.

James II's younger daughter Mary's second marriage was to John, Lord Hamilton and produced James, first Earl of Arran and Elizabeth who married Matthew Stewart, Earl of Lennox. There was an ongoing dispute between the two branches which would climax when a later Lennox, Lord Darnley was introduced to Mary, but at this time it was Arran who was regarded as Mary's heir presumptive. Arran was opposed to the treaty made at Haddington, as he had hoped that his own son might be a suitable husband for Mary. Although his dreams of a Hamilton-Stewart marriage appeared to be no longer obtainable, Arran was still Regent. In 1551 he was offered the dukedom of Châtelherault in France, along with an annual pension, which he accepted. In addition his son was to command the Scottish Guard in France; all this was in return for giving up the regency in Mary of Guise's favour.

Châtelherault's decision was not absolutely guaranteed as he might still have asked for assistance from the Protestant King Edward VI of England, but on Edward's death in July 1553, England was ruled by the Catholic Queen Mary which reduced the threat of renewed campaigns from south of the border. Arran accepted the bribe, but although his term of office was officially not due to end until Mary was 12 years old, he was however 'persuaded' to resign his post by April 1554. The Hamilton family by no means suffered as a result of this loss of position: his brother was then Archbishop of St Andrews, Châtelherault's son John was Commendator of Arbroath Abbey and Claud was Commendator of Paisley Abbey.

Arbroath Abbey

Commendators were originally clerics who administered and also acquired the revenues of religious benefices; by the sixteenth century, the posts were sometimes given to laymen who could enjoy the financial rewards without carrying out religious duties. Both financially and politically, the Hamiltons were to continue to play an important role in the future of Scotland.

As Regent, Mary of Guise attempted to carry out pro-French policies and co-operate with her native land in continuing the war against England. Several of her key administrative posts were given to Frenchmen – De Roubay was vice-chancellor and Villemore was comptroller, who shared financial administration with the treasurer. The French also maintained garrison posts at forts at Broughty, Dunbar and Inchkeith. Scottish finances were in deficit after Châtelherault's administration and Mary of Guise had some problems balancing the books. She gave her personal pension from France to her daughter in order to finance her expenses at the French court, so the Regent had to resort to an appeal to Rome for financial aid, as well as imposing several taxes on the Scottish people in order to meet the cost of warfare.

During this time, the religious question continued to be an important issue but both Mary of Guise and Archbishop Hamilton were more 'tolerant' than Beaton had been and Protestant preachers were not prosecuted or imprisoned. Mary needed the support of those nobles who expressed pro-Protestant, and possibly pro-English, tendencies in order to ensure that her daughter's marriage to the Dauphin would take place. At the same time as negotiations for the marriage were going on in 1557, several Protestant nobles signed a bond declaring their intention to overthrow the Catholic church. This *First Bond*, was signed in December 1557 by the Earls of Glencairn, Argyll, and Morton; Lord Lorne, son of Argyll; and John Erskine of Dun – but it did not attract as much support as was hoped and it would be another two years before the Protestant lords would take a more effective stance.

Meanwhile, Mary and François's wedding negotiations continued apace. Between December 1557 and April 1558 the French and Scots discussed the marriage settlement, and among the Scots commissioners sent to France by Mary of Guise were Lord James Stewart, Mary's half-brother, Erskine of Dun and Cassillis, two of whom had signed the *First Bond*. Because of his own problems with Spain Henri II was eager to hasten the final uniting of the two countries, but the Scots were still reluctant to acquiesce to all of France's proposals. The Scots wanted assurance of their country's liberties and laws, and were reluctant to acknowledge what might be perceived as France's suzerainty over Scotland: the authority of one sovereign over another sovereign, and thereby one state over another autonomous state – thereby recalling fears of similar attempts at domination by England. As well as national worries, the Hamiltons also wanted to ensure their right of inheritance to the Scottish crown if Mary were to have no children.

The French appeared to agree to these conditions. There was however another set of documents signed in secret three weeks before the wedding, which stated that the Scottish crown would pass to the French if Mary were childless, and that the kingdom of Scotland was to be put up as surety against the cost of her own personal expenses in France, and for any expenses which might be incurred by France in defending Scotland. The fact that four of the commissioners died before they returned to Scotland – and it would appear that they did not die of natural causes – has given rise to speculation that they may have found out about these secret agreements. The cause of their deaths has never been fully explained.

The remaining commissioners and the Scottish parliament were under the impression that they had conferred only the 'crown matrimonial' on François, but whatever was actually believed, the future appeared to indicate that Scotland would be governed by Mary and François from France. On 11 April 1558 Mary and François were officially betrothed in the Great Hall of the Louvre Palace in Paris, this event being followed by a lavish ball. The actual ceremony and more celebrations would take place on 24 April 1558.

Louvre Palace, Paris

4 – Wedding to widowhood

On 24 April 1558, a Sunday, the population of Paris swelled owing to the large number of visitors who had travelled to witness the royal wedding, due to take place in Notre Dame Cathedral. There were two versions of the marriage contract, and it would appear that the secret version was agreed to by Mary herself: the reasons for her agreeing may not have been simple political naiveté. Certainly Mary would have received much advice from her Guise-Lorraine relatives, and as marriage into the royal family of Valois would be to their advantage they would not see the signing away of the Scottish kingdom as a problem. Equally Mary was fond of, if perhaps not in love

Notre Dame Cathedral, Paris

with, François and marriage to him would bring benefit to herself and her kingdom, and as she was only 15 she would probably not consider the fact that she might die childless as likely.

The bride and groom were physically quite dissimilar. Mary was tall, elegant and personable, whereas François was small, unhealthy and did not have an endearing personality. The eldest child of Henri de Valois and the notorious Catherine de Medici was doted on by his parents. Henri and Catherine had had problems conceiving for some years, and as a result his mother was especially protective. Despite any failings that the cynics in the French court might ascribe to the Dauphin, the young couple appear to have been fond of each other.

The wedding was, despite any concerns which the Scots might have had, a great celebration. It was full of spectacle, music, colour and cheering. The bride and groom were dressed in expensive, magnificent clothes and bejewelled as was expected of queens and kings. Mary surprised French custom by appearing in a white dress. Traditionally, white was a mourning colour for the royal court in France, and brides usually wore silver, gold or purple. Mary also wore a gold crown covered with pearls, rubies and sapphires.

The wedding party proceeded from the Louvre to the Cathedral of Notre Dame, passing through the Paris crowds; and in keeping with the marriage customs of the time, the actual wedding vows were taken at the doors of the cathedral. There then followed a Mass inside. The festivities continued with a banquet and ball, and the general atmosphere of celebration continued for several months.

Mary was now queen of one country and the prospective queen of another and her future appeared bright and rosy. Mary even had a good relationship with her powerful mother-in-law who, because of her obsession with her son, many thought may have been jealous of Mary. Mary was a happy and likeable person compared to Catherine's scheming and plotting tendencies. Mary was also very tall, almost six feet, had auburn hair and a clear skin, and was regarded as quite a beauty. Catherine on the other hand was short, dark and older. But Mary and Catherine had a shared interest – the Dauphin's health and happiness, and the belief that he would eventually rule France as God's chosen divine monarch.

Added to the couple's claim to two royal titles, Henri II also announced that both François and Mary were the rightful heirs to the English crown. When Mary Tudor died she was succeeded by Elizabeth, Henry VIII's second daughter, who as a Protestant made it her objective to overturn her half-sister Mary Tudor's Catholic policies and re-introduce Protestant ones. As Rome had never regarded Henry as divorced from his first wife, any offspring born while Catharine of Aragon lived was regarded as illegitimate, especially one who was Protestant. As James IV had married Henry VIII's sister, Margaret Tudor, Mary had some claim to the English crown which Rome supported, and in which her father-in-law could also see political and economic advantages.

The situation in Scotland was still uncertain as the pro-French and pro-English parties fought for control. As Regent Mary of Guise's pro-French policies contributed to the revival of pro-English attitudes: either the result

of the presence of Frenchmen in the royal household and their perceived power, or her adoption of a more anti-Protestant stance than hitherto, or a combination of both. Discontent with the Catholic church grew among certain sections of the Scottish population, and found a voice by the end of 1558 and the beginning of 1559. In January the *Beggars' Summons* was nailed to the doors of friaries throughout the land. It stated that friars should leave, and hand over their goods and monies to the poor. There was an economic aspect to this document as much as a religious one. At the same time, Châtelherault, who was by this time pro-English, was in communication with the Englishman Sir Henry Percy, as the Protestants were concerned about the threat of a French Catholic invasion.

Despite, or because of, individual ambitions or fears, it was agreed between France, Spain and England to sign the Treaty of Cateau-Cambrésis in April 1559. By this agreement, there was to be a period of peace in Europe and a marriage between Princess Elisabeth de Valois, Mary's sister-in-law, and Philip II of Spain, and the celebrations to mark this betrothal were to be momentous in more than one way. Philip himself did not visit France and a proxy wedding was to be held in June, at which time the main festivities were to take place.

Henri II was very fond of jousting and so several jousting tournaments were arranged in which the king was to participate. Some time before the actual tournament, the astrologer Nostradamus told Catherine de Medici of a dream he had had. In the dream he saw a fight between two lions, one older than the other. The lions fought twice and in the second fight the young lion gouged out the eye of the older one, who died of the wound. Henri's escutcheon, his heraldic shield, was engraved with a lion. Catherine, along with many others of that time, believed in divination through a variety of methods and it may have been that she believed Nostradamus's prophecy – she was not, however, able to persuade her husband against taking part. Clothed in black and white, the colours of his mistress Diane de Poitiers, Henri successfully jousted three times. He is then reported to have challenged one of his opponents to a second bout but on this occasion his opponent's lance broke, a splinter going into the king's eye. Attended by his family, Henri died from his wound ten days later and François was declared king of France.

Henri II was buried at St Denis and François crowned at Rheims in September 1559. There now began a power struggle for control over the young king – his mother against his uncles-in-law, the Guises. François was entirely unsuited to, or perhaps unready for, his regal responsibilities; and showed little interest in affairs of state, preferring to spend time hunting, which he enjoyed with a passion despite his poor physique. Mary's uncles attempted to persuade the king to attend to his duties, but with little success. His mother began to shift her attention to her second son, Charles, as a possible heir to the throne if François and Mary produced no children, and one whom she would be able to control without interference from the Guise faction. François and Mary found themselves caught in an unenviable position: the freedom and innocence of their childhood had quickly passed.

Mary, portrait by François Clouet

Pressures on Mary increased as any possible signs of pregnancy were looked for with anticipation; which added to the increasingly disturbing news from Scotland. Religious problems had increased for the Regent as more Scottish nobles joined the Protestant cause. After Mary became Queen of France more French troops were sent to Scotland and garrisoned at Leith. In October the Protestant lords, headed by Châtelherault, marched on Edinburgh and proceeded to suspend Mary of Guise from the Regency. This provisional government may have held the capital of the country, but it lacked the capital required to administer and further their cause, and by November they had to evacuate to Stirling after an unsuccessful attack on Leith. Mary of Guise re-took Edinburgh and restored Catholic Mass in the city. The next couple of months resulted in stalemate as it became clear that neither group would be able to take power without outside help. English help was requested by the Protestant party and as Fife was held as a stronghold by the French, the English fleet sailed north in order to cut their communication route with the French mainland.

The French still held Leith, but in February 1560 the Treaty of Berwick was signed between Elizabeth of England and the Scottish Protestants, Elizabeth having promised to help their rebellion against Mary of Guise and to assist their campaign against the French. The siege of Leith had begun by the end of March 1560 but it was soon clear that it was not going to end quickly. Mary of Guise moved into Edinburgh Castle as a safer alternative to Holyrood Palace on 1 April, but she was not to see the end of the siege as she died, of dropsy, an accumulation of body fluid, on 11 June. Her death enabled the hostilities to end but was not necessarily to make things easier for her daughter.

The Treaty of Edinburgh was signed on 6 July 1560 and it was agreed that both the English and French troops would withdraw from Scotland, and François and Mary would give up their claim to the English crown and recognize Elizabeth as rightful queen of England. The following month the Scottish parliament accepted a reformed Confession of Faith, rejected papal authority and forbade the practice of the Mass; and in order to give authority to their actions they asked François and Mary to ratify these acts. Mary, grieving in France, had more loss ahead.

Her Guise relatives needed to find a suitable Regent for Scotland who could hold back the tide of Scottish protestantism, but unfortunately another crisis changed their plans. After a day's hunting in November 1560 François returned complaining of a sore ear. Earache was one of his frequent ailments and little was thought of it. Surely it was only the cold autumn weather which had exacerbated an old infection? But there was a rumour that François was so disliked by his people, poison had been poured into his ear while he slept. After fainting, François developed a fever and despite being nursed continually by his wife and his mother, the infection spread to his brain and he died on the 5 December. Mary was now a widow and no longer Queen of France. Her powerful mother-in-law took over the running of the state, on behalf of Charles IX, François's younger brother, and Mary's immediate future was uncertain.

5 – Return to Scotland

Ce qui m'était plaisant
Ores m'est peine dure
Le jour le plus luisant
M'est nuit noire et obscure;
Et n'est rien si exquis
Qui de moi soit requis

Throughout her life Mary turned to poetry to enable her to find expression for her emotions, and this *Ode sur la mort, de son mari, Le Roi François II (Ode on the death of her husband, King Francis II)* fully expressed her grief and loss. This stanza describes metaphorically the loss of her husband as the loss of light in her life, which is now as dark as night.

Mary wore the white of mourning that was expected of royalty, and embarked on forty days of isolation from public view. Apart from coming to terms with her own personal loss, Mary was urged by her relatives to make plans for her future. She was free to remain in France, where she now had no official position, or she could return to Scotland, where she could govern as monarch in her own right. Rumours soon started about who and when she would remarry, rumours which were to follow her throughout her life. There were candidates aplenty – rich, poor, princes, kings, nobles – many were considered in secret by Mary and her relatives, but all were dismissed except the heir to the throne of Spain, Don Carlos. François may have been fragile but Don Carlos was no great improvement. Slight of build, suffering from epilepsy and a speech impediment, marriage to Don Carlos would appear to have been one of dynastic advantage, wealth and honour rather than attraction. The dynastic possibilities – which would give Spain, one of France's old rivals, a useful ally – were such that when Catherine de Medici discovered the plans, she persuaded Philip II of Spain, through her daughter Elisabeth, that alliance with Scotland would be a dangerous and expensive venture. By spring 1561 the Spanish match was off.

The alternative of staying in France, without any official status, in a court controlled entirely by Catherine de Medici – who had now no reason to be amicable to her daughter-in-law – was not a particularly attractive option. Mary began to consider the feasibility of returning to the land of her birth. The danger, of which her advisors warned her, was that Scotland was now, to all intents and purposes, Protestant and Mary, as a Catholic monarch, would have difficulties governing unless she managed to drive out the controlling Protestants. But Mary, who had received formal invitations to return from her half-brother Lord James Stewart and the Scottish parliament, was less concerned about possible dangers, and increasingly aware that Scotland and the Scots were hers by birth. She was conscious that it was her responsibility to govern now that the country lacked any official Regent. Another advantage was that she would not have to worry about her scheming mother-in-law.

Although the death of François had posed dynastic problems for Mary, in Scotland the concerns of those governing the country continued to be more about the Protestant settlement and church organization. The *Book of Discipline*, the statement of reformed church policy, had taken some time to compile, and even by January 1561 its acceptance by nobles and lairds was only qualified. The reformed church attempted to set up organization both at parish and higher level, but as a wider system of presbyteries would not appear until later, at this time supervision of the parishes was to be done by superintendents. An embryonic form of assembly met in December 1560 and April 1562, but the *Book of Discipline* had not clarified the formal relationship between church and state; was the state to have authority over the church or could the church develop an independent role from the state? These questions would remain at issue for many years.

It should be remembered that opinion in Scotland was divided, and that there were still areas of major disagreement. The possible return of Mary met with varied response – those who might still be classed as Catholic welcomed the plan, others felt that Mary should only return if she agreed to marry the Protestant son of Châtelherault, James, third Earl of Arran. Yet another alternative was that Mary should be allowed to return without having to compromise her religious beliefs, as long as she did not try to further a Catholic cause using foreign support.

An important aspect of the machinations behind negotiations was as ever the importance of relations between England and Scotland. Elizabeth was still unmarried, having recently rejected the offer of the Earl of Arran, and therefore Mary still had a claim to the English crown. If Elizabeth could be assured that Mary did not intend to start a Catholic revival, then perhaps Elizabeth would name Mary as her official heir. Lord James Stewart was sent to France with the Scottish offer and he advocated taking the third option, so Mary might return to Scotland, and remain faithful to her chosen religion, as long as she did so in private.

Mary was in the north-east of France, with her Guise relatives, away from the pressures of the royal court, when Lord James arrived to open formal negotiations on behalf of the Scottish parliament. Mary, possibly still in a state of grief and confusion, appeared to welcome the solid advice of her half-brother. She may have been loyal to the Catholic faith, but she was also pragmatic and adaptable, especially when there were few alternatives available to her. Although the official offer from Scotland had come through Lord James, Mary had received another possible route for her return from the Catholic Earl of Huntly. Huntly had offered to raise troops in the north, to support her and force the rest of the country to convert, if she would sail directly to the north rather than Edinburgh. Mary demonstrated a maturing political awareness by rejecting Huntly's offer, and agreed to a policy of toleration and conciliation, both for Scottish Protestants and for herself. She wanted assurance that she would be allowed to attend Mass and take Catholic communion in private with no interference. This was settled and Mary made preparations to leave France.

In the sixteenth century, travel in foreign lands required guarantees for safe conduct, and therefore as a formality, Mary applied to Elizabeth for safe passage through English waters. Elizabeth was not satisfied that Mary had fully ratified the terms of the Treaty of Edinburgh, and so there was a delay after Elizabeth initially refused Mary's request. Mary left Paris on the 25 July 1561, and set off for Calais accompanied by three uncles, friends,

Lamb's House, Leith (see next page)

household servants and of course, the four Marys. By 14 August, although no official safe conduct had been received from Elizabeth, Mary decided that she could no longer hold off her departure, and despite anxieties about possible interceptions by English ships, Mary and her entourage set off into a misty horizon.

On 18 August, two ships were spotted off the coast flying blue flags bearing the French royal coat of arms. By the next day, the ships had reached the Firth of Forth and they sailed into Leith harbour at about nine o'clock in the morning. A typical Edinburgh sight welcomed the returning Queen – a dense haar rising off the Firth of Forth obscured any view of the city. Although the Scots knew her arrival was imminent, Mary had arrived sooner than expected and so as the royal party disembarked Mary was greeted by a relatively small crowd of local people and a few officials.

The sight of their queen, dressed in mourning but accompanied by her colourfully dressed party, posed the local officials with a dilemma of protocol, as they had no idea where to take her or what to do with her. No contingency plans had been made, so Lamb's House, the house of a local merchant Andrew Lamb, was requisitioned for her use. There she could rest while messages were sent to Edinburgh. The Scottish nobility began to descend on Lamb's House by the afternoon and after some refreshment, escorted by her nobles, Mary travelled to Holyrood Palace. The way was lined with a cheering crowd welcoming her home, pleased by the sight of their pretty young queen who herself appeared delighted by the warmth of the crowds. If Mary had doubts about her decision to return to Scotland when she first arrived, they were dispersed by this joyous, enthusiastic support.

Mary was serenaded by the Edinburgh crowds during her first night at Holyrood, and Alexander Scott composed the poem *Ane New Yeir Gift* to commemorate her arrival

> *Welcum, illustrat Ladye, and oure Quene;*
> *Welcum oure lyone, with the 'Fleur-de-lyce';*
> *Welcum oure thrissill, with the 'Lorane' grene;*
> *Welcum oure rubent rois upoun the ryce;*
> *Welcum oure jem and joyful genetryce;*
> *Welcum oure beill of 'Albion' to beir;*
> *Welcum oure plesand Princès, maist of pryce;*
> *God gif ye grace aganis this guid new-yeir*
> (Alexander Scott, 1561)

The following Sunday, Mary attended Mass at the Chapel Royal at Holyrood Palace conducted by a French priest. When the Edinburgh citizens heard of this a less than friendly crowd gathered outside and attacked a royal servant.

Holyrood Palace

The uproar drew the attention of Lord James, who true to his promise of allowing Mary religious freedom in the privacy of her household, persuaded the crowd to disperse. John Knox was to declare that this action indicated that Lord James had abandoned the Protestant cause, which was very much an exaggeration and typical of Knox's emotive rhetoric. In Mary's first proclamation as Queen of Scots she announced that she would not allow any change in the current state of religion in the country, thus permitting Protestant worship, but she maintained her right to participate in private Catholic worship.

Mary's formal welcome to the Scottish capital included dinner at the castle, followed by a procession down the Royal Mile to Holyrood Palace. This spectacle was in similar vein to some of the festivities that Mary had seen in France. She was carried in a purple, gold fringed canopy preceded by 50 men disguised as moors, wearing black masks, black capes and yellow suits. There were maidens dressed as the Virtues, while others re-enacted mythological and religious legends. Cannon were fired from the castle, there was music and singing and welcoming speeches. The pageant also contained more subtle messages to Mary. A child, painted in gold, descended from a cloud and presented her with the symbolic keys to the city and two velvet covered books. One was the Bible, in English, and the other the Protestant service book. These clear symbols of the reformed faith spoilt the celebrations for Mary, and she summoned to Holyrood the man who she felt was the instigator of these *insults*. This was to be the first of several encounters with the man who for many is the image of Scottish protestantism and the Reformation – John Knox.

6 – Mary's personal rule

Although she may have intended to permit freedom of worship for her Protestant subjects, Mary also felt that to an extent, as a rightful monarch, she should have some authority over the spiritual comfort of her subjects. She also had some insight into the fact that religious unrest could turn to civil unrest, and was anxious to avoid this possibility. The Queen therefore agreed to meet John Knox.

The extreme wing of the Protestants had been led by the Earl of Arran, whose own motives were in fact inspired by his thwarted ambition to marry Mary. As this plan was repeatedly rejected, Arran began to show signs of mental imbalance and he was eventually confined from 1562 until he died in 1609. Arran's motives may have been more than religious, but that cannot be said of another leader of the group.

Knox had been a follower of George Wishart, the Protestant preacher burnt by Cardinal Beaton, and had been involved in the siege of St Andrews Castle, after which he was sent to France as punishment. On his release, he went to England and preached successfully there until the reign of Mary Tudor. Mary Tudor's anti-Protestant campaign forced Knox to flee to Geneva for safety, but he returned to Scotland in 1559 to join in the overthrow of Mary of Guise and the Catholics. Knox's preaching was noted for its vehement anti-Catholic sentiment and on occasion, notably in Perth, led to riot and iconoclasm, when church carvings and other Catholic icons were destroyed. Knox was appointed minister of Edinburgh on 7 July 1559 but, using his noted powers of self preservation, removed himself when it looked as if Mary of Guise might hold onto the Regency. On Queen Mary's arrival, having returned to Edinburgh, he preached a sermon against her taking Mass, even although she had been guaranteed this privilege.

Their first meeting took place after this sermon and Mary, perhaps because she had been brought up to expect to certain degree of respect for her position of authority as a woman of royal birth, probably did not expect to hear arguments, which were both anti-Catholic and anti-female, directed at her. She may have thought that she was able to hold her own in discussions of a religious or political nature, but she had never before encountered such a man and was unable to win him round as she had hoped. Knox unsettled Mary greatly by implying that if subjects were ruled by a Catholic monarch, then it was their duty to God to disobey that monarch. The interview was not a success, but the ground rules were laid by the two protagonists which neither would be willing to change.

Mary may have been unsettled by Knox's clear religious intolerance but she had no intention of embarking on a campaign to enforce Scotland to renounce protestantism. Her attitude towards the Protestant church, as well as her reassurances to Rome, show that Mary was quite canny and sensible. Some have suggested that her motives were those of self-interest and opportunism, which may be a little harsh. Given the standards and motives of behaviour of most monarchs of the time, Mary's actions to ensure her self-preservation were no better and no worse. Realizing the power of the Protestants, Mary re-affirmed her intention that while she could take Mass privately, priests would not be permitted to say Mass elsewhere. She also granted the reformed church money from major benefices in February 1562. In theory, the revenues from the benefices went to the holders, but Mary ordained that one third was to be divided between the government and the reformed church.

It was clear that in order to survive, Mary had to play a game of reconciliation and compromise. Mary worked with her Protestant nobles, acknowledging that it was better to have them on her side than against her. To this end, she even made it clear that she rejected the counsel and advice of those who had Catholic tendencies. Mary governed the country through her privy council, which was at this time mostly Protestant. She attended meetings and listened to the debates of her nobles, contributing to the discussion when needed. On the other hand, Mary's household was largely made up of those who had accompanied her from France: the four Marys, musicians, poets, dancers, chefs and physicians. She was able to participate in the style of courtly life which she had enjoyed in France, albeit on a smaller scale. She could listen to the music of David Rizzio and the poetry of Pierre de Châtelard. Both of them played future roles in less pleasant circumstances, but in the meantime provided Mary with much enjoyable diversion.

The royal court did provide some opportunity for the mixing of Mary's Protestant Scottish nobles and her predominantly Catholic household, but Mary had another group whose support and welcome she quickly realized would be important to her. This was of course the Scottish people themselves. Having experienced life at the peripatetic French court, she had seen that moving around a country would give both monarch and subjects opportunities to see each other. Public journeys throughout the country would enable her to display her political strength and govern her kingdom, as the privy council could travel with her. Also Mary remembered little of her country of birth and these progresses allowed her to see her kingdom more fully, as well as removing her from Edinburgh and John Knox. Between 1562 and 1565 two-thirds of the time were spent on royal progresses; between August 1562 and September 1563 she covered 1200 miles and 460 miles between July and September 1564.

The first progress, between 10 August 1562 and 21 November 1562, took Mary to Linlithgow Palace where she had been born. From there she travelled to Stirling, Perth, Coupar Angus, Glamis Castle owned by the Lyon family, Edzell Castle property of the Lindsays, and Aberdeen. She then

Edzell Castle

progressed to the Earl of Moray's castle at Darnaway in Moray, Inverness, Spynie Palace which was the property of the Bishop of Moray, Aberdeen again and the Keith castle at Dunnottar. Next she visited Montrose in Angus, Dundee, another visit to Stirling and finally back to Edinburgh. She also stayed at the Earl of Atholl's castle at Balvenie in the September and Arbroath Abbey, in the Abbot's House, in November of that year. The progress started well, but at Stirling, as she was hearing Mass at the Chapel Royal, there was a scuffle inside the chapel involving her half-brother, Lord James. At Perth, although there was a cheering crowd to welcome her, some of the pageants performed had similar anti-Catholic meanings to the Edinburgh ones. This appeared to upset Mary and reportedly caused her to faint. In 1562 Mary also visited Crichton Castle, property of the Hepburns, to attend the wedding of her half-brother Lord James to Lady Janet Hepburn.

Part of the progress was to the region of the north-east of Scotland where the Gordon family was very powerful. George Gordon, fourth Earl of Huntly, was an extremely powerful man in his locality, as well as nationally. He was lieutenant in the north, sheriff of Aberdeen, owned and administered large areas of land and was known to have Catholic sympathies. Indeed, he had suggested that Mary land at Aberdeen to start a Catholic administration in 1561. Mary had rejected this plan and while this may have contributed to Huntly's annoyance with her, it may also have been Mary's decision about the earldoms of Mar and Moray that really displeased Huntly.

Huntly had been administering and benefiting from these lands until 1562, when Mary decided to grant the titles and lands to Lord James. This probably did not increase her popularity with the Gordons, although Sir John Gordon, Huntly's third son, had some plans to persuade Mary of his suitability to be her husband. When Mary reached Inverness, the captain of

Balvenie Castle (see previous page)

the town, who was Lord Gordon, Huntly's oldest son, refused her entry. Mary's troops rallied to her side and took the garrison; Lord Gordon was then executed as punishment for his insolence.

Huntly and Sir John Gordon assembled the Gordon forces, intending to block Mary's progress to Aberdeen: she was however allowed to pass. Huntly was summoned to appear before the privy council to explain his actions, but as he failed to appear he was put to 'the horn' which meant he was declared outlawed and forfeited. Huntly marched on Aberdeen but Mary's forces, led by Lord James, now the Earl of Moray, and Maitland of Lethington, met up with the Gordons at Corrichie, near Aberdeen, on 28 October 1562. The battle in the end was quick and the Gordon forces completely routed. Prior to the battle, the elderly Huntly is reported to have been reluctant to engage in combat, and when he was captured he took a sudden seizure, possibly a stroke, and died. Legend says that he may have died of apoplexy, but whatever the diagnosis, the Gordons lost much as a result of Corrichie. Sir John was executed and Huntly was posthumously convicted of treason and forfeited. The Gordon castle at Huntly was sacked as part of the punishment.

Huntly Castle

1563 was to bring its own problems for Mary. Plans were made for another progress, this time a smaller one to Fife. No matter what political issues were proving problematic or that there were yet more reports of Knox's repeated accusations of her Catholic idolatry, Mary was reassured by the obvious pleasure that her subjects expressed when they saw her. Despite taking action against what might have been perceived as a Catholic plot, Mary still had to appease the reformers more. To this end there were several prosecutions for saying Mass, Mary did not give an audience to the Jesuit de Gouda and she did not send Scottish representatives to the meetings of the Council of Trent, the forum for discussion between Rome and the reformers, organized by the Catholic church. There was also the growing speculation, associated with any unmarried monarch, about possible suitors

– occupied not only the Scottish people and the nobles, but also Mary herself. The possibility of a match with Don Carlos of Spain was again discussed, as without the interference of Catherine de Medici, Mary's own Scottish ambassadors could undertake negotiations.

These issues remained among Mary's concerns as she set off on 11 February 1563 to Rossend Castle, near Burntisland. Members of her household travelled with her, amongst them Pierre de Châtelard, a young French poet whose admiration of the Queen had turned to infatuation and passion. In an incident at Holyrood, following a masque where the closest members of Mary's court dressed up in clothes of the opposite sex, Châtelard was found concealed under Mary's bed by her attendants. Mary was very upset and angry, and ordered the poet to leave her court. As there were no attempts to ensure that he had obeyed the queen's orders, Châtelard was still with the queen's household when it arrived at Burntisland.

In the evening, when Mary retired to her bedchamber, he followed her and forced his way in, to find her being disrobed by two of her Marys. There he made physical advances to her until the Earl of Moray, Lord James, came to her aid. These two episodes were fuel for the fires of rumour- and scandal-mongers, and Châtelard had to be dealt with severely in order to maintain the queen's dignity. After being imprisoned he was tried and executed at St Andrews, where before he died he quoted from Ronsard's poem *Hymn to Death*. Despite the attempts at damage limitation, Knox still managed to use these incidents in his continued criticism of Mary.

The progress through Fife continued from St Andrews to the royal palace at Falkland and then back to Edinburgh by the 18 May, and as she went round the country debate continued about Mary's possible marriage. There was no doubt that she wanted to re-marry, but she was aware that whoever was chosen had to be acceptable to more than just herself and her council. Her French relatives continued to advise her by letter, still hoping for a powerful Catholic union; and there was also the small matter of Mary's claim as heir to the English crown.

Elizabeth had neither married, nor named her chosen heir. Mary was well aware that any marriage might influence Elizabeth's decision, and therefore she sent Maitland of Lethington to negotiate with Elizabeth on her behalf. The stumbling block, as far as Elizabeth was concerned, was that Mary had thus far refused to ratify the Treaty of Edinburgh, in which Mary would agreed to refrain from calling herself Queen of England. Mary, for her part, used the excuse that she could not ratify any treaty without the consent

Map 3: 1563 (Chapter 6)

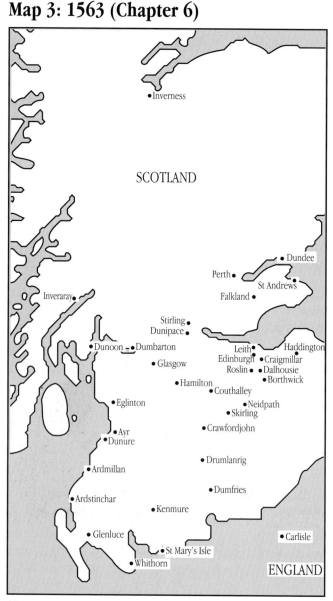

SCOTLAND

- Inverness
- Dundee
- Perth
- St Andrews
- Falkland
- Inveraray
- Stirling
- Dunipace
- Dunoon – Dumbarton
- Leith
- Haddington
- Edinburgh
- Craigmillar
- Glasgow
- Roslin
- Dalhousie
- Borthwick
- Hamilton
- Couthalley
- Eglinton
- Neidpath
- Skirling
- Ayr
- Crawfordjohn
- Dunure
- Ardmillan
- Drumlanrig
- Ardstinchar
- Dumfries
- Kenmure
- Glenluce
- Carlisle
- St Mary's Isle
- Whithorn

ENGLAND

of her parliament, which of course had not met since she had returned. International discussions about the possible Spanish marriage were to continue, much to the annoyance of Elizabeth, who played her trump card of the English succession – if Mary would marry someone of her choice then Elizabeth might agree to name Mary as her heir. As early as spring 1563 Elizabeth suggested as a possible match Robert Dudley, later created Earl of Leicester, who – it was rumoured – was Elizabeth's lover.

On the 1 July 1563 Mary set out on another progress, this time to the west, Dumfries and Galloway and the borders. From Edinburgh she travelled to Dunipace, Glasgow, Hamilton centre of the Hamilton family lands, then to Dumbarton Castle and to Inveraray Castle, centre of the Campbell Earl of Argyll, another of her Protestant nobles. She then moved to Dunoon, and Eglington, stronghold of the Montgomery Earls of Eglington. Hugh Montgomery, the third earl, was a devout Catholic who remained loyal to Mary throughout her reign. Next, she progressed south along the coast to Ayr and then to Dunure, owned by the Kennedys, Earls of Cassillis, another loyal Catholic family. Travelling further south Mary moved to Ardmillan and Ardstinchar held by the Kennedys of Bargany. The entourage then headed to the Abbey of Glenluce and the Priory of Whithorn, both well known

Whithorn Priory

religious sites and pilgrimage routes. Next stop was Kenmure Castle, owned by the Gordons, Viscounts of Kenmure, St Mary's Isle and then Dumfries. Moving north Mary then called at Drumlanrig Castle property of the Douglas family and Crawfordjohn owned by the Hamiltons, Couthalley owned by the Somervilles, then the Cockburn stronghold of Skirling Castle. The next port of call was at Neidpath Castle, near Peebles, owned by the Hays. Then Borthwick, south of Edinburgh, followed by Dalhousie held by the Ramsays and Roslin, the property of the Sinclairs of Roslin. The progress ended back in Edinburgh in September 1563 after a visit to Craigmillar Castle just outside the city. It is clear from her itinerary that Mary was careful to show no obvious preference between Protestant and Catholic families and attempted to balance her favours.

By the middle of 1564 the possible marriage between Don Carlos and Mary was finally called off, due to the Spanish prince's insanity, and in July Mary once again set off on her travels. In England Elizabeth and her advisors continued to discuss other possible husbands for Mary. This progress between 21 July and 15 September took Mary to Linlithgow again followed by Perth, Blair Castle the Earl of Atholl's stronghold, Inverness, Gartly Castle property of the Barclays, Aberdeen and Dundee. Elizabeth continued to plead for Lord Dudley as a possible husband for Mary, but although Maitland was in discussions about the match, it was the appearance at court of another young man who was ultimately to play an important role in the fate of Mary and Scotland.

7 – Love and marriage

The exiled Earl of Lennox appealed to Mary to be allowed to return to Scotland. When she agreed to this she upset several of her loyal Protestant nobles, not least Châtelherault and the rest of the Hamiltons, as the Lennoxes had a shared dynastic claim to the throne with the Hamiltons. Equally upsetting was the fact that he was a Catholic; but it was his son Henry, Lord Darnley, who would prove to have a devastating effect on Mary and her future. Darnley was brought up by his mother, Lady Margaret Douglas, to be a fine sportsman, well versed in courtly refinements and expected by his mother to be a possible suitor first for Elizabeth, and later Mary. Darnley was tall and good looking and when Elizabeth saw him at court, she took quickly to the idea of Darnley as Mary's suitor instead of Dudley.

Darnley arrived in Scotland in the beginning of 1565 and Mary first met him at Wemyss Castle on the 16 February during another of her progresses. This journey between 16 January and 24 February 1565 included Falkland, the Balfour Castle at Collairnie near Cupar, Ballinbreich Castle, owned by the Leslies, near Newburgh, Balmerino Abbey and St Andrews. She then travelled to Struthers, a property owned by the Lindsays of The Byres, followed by Lundin Tower near Lower Largo and Durie, and finally to Wemyss Castle. Before returning to Edinburgh Mary called at Dunfermline, staying at the abbey there. Initially relations between Mary and Darnley were very much those of monarch and subject, and

Balmerino Abbey

Map 4: 1564-5 (Chapter 7)

Darnley was extremely courteous and respectful, which pleased Mary. After a visit to Dunkeld, to visit his father, he re-joined the Queen as she returned to Edinburgh and became a constant member of the royal court.

Darnley made every effort to charm Mary by dancing and singing, and generally participating in all the courtly pursuits which Mary so enjoyed. Darnley and David Rizzio got on very well together, which pleased Mary, and Darnley also shared Mary's enjoyment of hunting. It is not clear if Mary was already planning to marry Darnley, but when Elizabeth suddenly announced that if Mary was to marry Dudley she would lose her claim to the English throne, Mary was very upset and felt that she had been used by Elizabeth. Whatever her motives, she turned her attention to Darnley as a possible suitor.

This plan certainly ruffled many feathers. Mary may have believed that a marriage to Darnley would strengthen her claim to the English throne, and indeed privately Elizabeth may have seen it as a better alternative than marriage to a continental Catholic, but this was not her reported public reaction. Nor did Mary's nobles feel that this was a wise move, and after she spent some time nursing Darnley through a bout of measles in April 1565, some of her most loyal Protestant nobles – Moray, Lord James, Châtelherault, Glencairn, Morton and Ruthven, signed a bond agreeing to join together to prevent the marriage. The motives behind the signing of this bond may have had as much to do with dislike of Lennox, and fear of his possible increase in power, as the unsuitability of the marriage.

By May, Moray made his opinion about the match obvious to Mary, and Argyll refused to attend the convention which discussed, and eventually agreed to, Mary's wishes. Later that month, Mary created Darnley Earl of Ross; Lord Robert Stewart was created Earl of Orkney and Shetland, and in June, Lord Erskine was raised to the earldom of Mar. It might be said that with the loss of some of her most senior nobles, Mary was attempting to create a second line of defence.

Mary issued a proclamation in July, in reply to a supplication from her subjects, and declared that she did not intend to interfere with matters of religion; and at the same time she requested a papal dispensation from Rome to permit the marriage to Darnley. This was because she and Darnley were, as blood relatives, and according to church rules, too closely related. In the end, Mary did not wait until the dispensation arrived and rumours abounded that this was because she was already Darnley's mistress. Society has always indulged in gossip about the rich and famous, and sixteenth-century Scotland was no exception. Even ministers of the church, especially

Family Tree of Mary

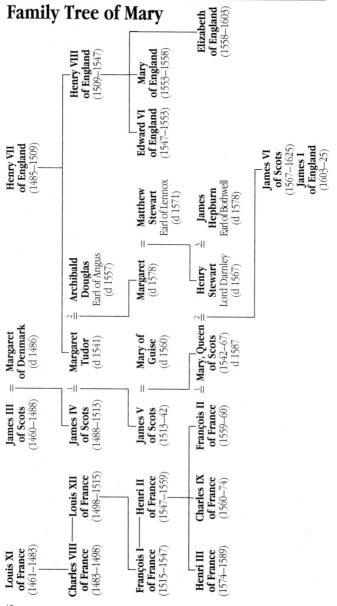

Henry VII of England (1485–1509)

Henry VIII of England (1509–1547)

Edward VI of England (1547–1553)

Mary of England (1553–1558)

Elizabeth of England (1558–1603)

Margaret of Denmark (d 1486)

James III of Scots (1460–1488) =

James IV of Scots (1488–1513) =¹

Margaret Tudor (d 1541) ²= Archibald Douglas Earl of Angus (d 1557)

James V of Scots (1513–42) = Mary of Guise (d 1560)

Margaret (d 1578) = Matthew Stewart Earl of Lennox (d 1571)

Louis XI of France (1461–1483)

Charles VIII of France (1483–1498) —— Louis XII of France (1498–1515)

François I of France (1515–1547) —— Henri II of France (1547–1559)

François II of France (1559–60) =¹ Mary, Queen of Scots (1542–67) d 1587 ²= Henry Stewart Lord Darnley (d 1567)

³= James Hepburn Earl of Bothwell (d 1578)

Charles IX of France (1560–74)

Henri III of France (1574–1589)

James VI of Scots (1567–1625) James I of England (1603–25)

Knox, thought fit to comment on the rumours about Mary's sex life.

Once Mary had received tacit agreement from her French relatives, Philip of Spain and Charles IX of France, she could wait no longer and on 16 July Mary and Darnley rode to Seton Palace, stronghold of Lord Seton, a Catholic supporter of Mary. The couple stayed two nights there, adding to the public rumours, before they returned to Edinburgh. The following Sunday, the banns, or proclamations, were announced for their forthcoming wedding, which was to take place on the 19 July 1565. During the intervening days, Mary made it clear that the opposition to her choice of husband displeased her greatly. There were rumours that Darnley had plotted against Moray, but Moray had actually started these rumours himself. Mary could see no obstacle to the wedding, and even the question of Darnley's religion was not an issue. Darnley, although his mother was Catholic, had professed the reformed faith in England, so he did not attend the wedding Mass and attended services at St Giles led by Knox.

Early in the morning of Sunday 29 July, Mary, dressed in black as a sign of her widowhood, was escorted from her chambers at Holyrood Palace to the private chapel. As part of the ceremony, Darnley placed three rings on Mary's finger, after which they were blessed by the priest. Darnley then left his bride to her private Mass. On her return to her apartments, her attendants removed her black widow's dress which they replaced with a new brightly-coloured gown, symbolizing a new stage in her life. The wedding celebrations, although perhaps not as sumptuous as those she had experienced in France, were merry and lavish. Eating, drinking, music and dancing were enjoyed by the guests, and handfuls of gold coins were thrown to the watching crowds.

Before her marriage Mary had declared that Darnley was to be referred to as King of Scots, a title which she was not legally entitled to grant, and which added to the nobles' displeasure with Darnley. When Moray, summoned to appear before her to explain his behaviour, failed to appear Mary declared him 'put to the horn', and officially declared outlaw. This was the start of what was to be known as the *Chaseabout Raid*.

Moray and the other rebels made for Argyll, and Mary announced that any who provided them with aid would be punished. The rebels appealed to Elizabeth for assistance, using the ready excuse of the reformed religion as a common cause, as well as stressing the dangers associated with Darnley's recent promotion. Whether Mary had found new confidence with her recent marriage, or whether she was actually fearful that the Protestant rebels might succeed is not clear but she responded quickly during this crisis. She made it clear that she was not willing to lose all that she had so recently gained, and, summoning her troops, she set out to quash the rebellion. Mary also ordered Edinburgh town council to depose its Protestant provost and she replaced him with Sir Simon Preston of Craigmillar, who was to prove one of her most loyal supporters in later years.

Mary headed towards Stirling as the rebels – Châtelherault and Moray and approximately 2000 men – arrived in Edinburgh, but they found little support there and so made for the south-west and Dumfries, hoping that Elizabeth might have sent help north. Mary, after a visit to the Ruthven castle, later called Huntingtower, near Perth, returned to Edinburgh by 22 September where she hoped to raise more support. Having put Châtelherault and the others, as well as Moray, to the horn, Mary followed them to Dumfries, ready to resolve the situation by combat if required. By the 8 October, Mary and her forces had arrived at Dumfries, from where she and Darnley attended a banquet at Lochmaben Castle on 14 October, but Moray had already crossed the border

16th-century painted ceiling, Huntingtower Castle

once he realized that there was to be no English help. Indeed, Elizabeth later even refused to grant any of the rebels an audience. It was at Dumfries that Mary met another man, who was later to be an important influence on her. The Earl of Bothwell had recently returned from exile, and Mary made him her lieutenant-general when he joined her campaign.

The *Chaseabout Raid* may not have been an auspicious start to a new marriage, but it showed Mary at her most effective and regal – able to respond as the situation demanded, and also able to command a good amount of popular support from the ordinary people of Scotland. The marriage to Darnley may have made some Scots unhappy, but it appeared that the majority supported her, which would have reassured her. Mary returned to Edinburgh and set about the business of governing her kingdom with, she hoped, the support of her husband. The peers of the realm who were now Mary's supporters were Huntly, Atholl, Lennox and Bothwell; other posts were filled with non-Scots or others not of noble birth. Nevertheless Mary hoped that things would soon settle down. However, it became obvious quite quickly that Darnley was unsuited for his responsibilities, either because he was too young or because he was not interested. Instead of being a help to Mary, he began to be a hindrance.

Map 5: 1566–8 (Chapters 8–10)

8 – Pregnancies and plots

Darnley was annoyed with Mary for giving the position of lieutenant-general to Bothwell, and this resulted in a violent disagreement, one of many, between the couple. Darnley displayed little interest in affairs of state or the responsibilities of government. He even felt that Mary spent too much time on these issues. She was therefore reluctant to grant him the crown matrimonial, which would have meant that the crown would pass to his family if she should predecease him. Unfortunately, official royal documents required both their signatures, and because Darnley was absent so often from meetings Mary had a stamp made of his signature which could be used in his absence. Darnley's childish behaviour was not only troublesome to Mary, but provided her enemies with ammunition to use against her about her own unfitness to reign. Whatever the relationship was between the royal couple, things may have remained manageable, especially once Mary discovered she was pregnant. A legitimate heir to the crown of Scotland would be a great boost to morale and a pointed message to Elizabeth in England who was, as yet, unmarried.

Mary was in the early stages of pregnancy after the *Chaseabout Raid* and an episode of illness had given rise to rumours, but it was not until she chose to travel back to Edinburgh by carriage, rather than her customary horseback, that the rumour became official. This news may have been welcomed by most, but there were some who were not so pleased, particularly the Hamiltons. Darnley, because of his arrogance and immaturity, became a useful weapon for Mary's enemies. As he became increasingly distant from Mary, and she from him, the Queen's enemies sowed seeds of doubt in his mind – why would she not grant him the crown matrimonial giving him equal rights? Mary was a woman and as such was secondary to her husband and should respect him. Who did she spend her time with when Darnley was out drinking?

This last question was also on the lips of many others and the answer, many felt, was obvious – David Rizzio, Mary's Italian secretary. Rizzio had arrived at Mary's court as a musician, but having attracted Mary's attention, his desire for promotion resulted in his appointment as her secretary. In this position, he naturally spent much time in Mary's company and certainly appeared to have some influence over her. This may simply have been because he was both good company and also listened to Mary's problems, perhaps providing the emotional support that should have come from her husband.

This position of proximity to, and the confidence of, the Queen gave rise to both jealousy in Darnley and fears in Mary's enemies – the Earls Moray, Morton, Argyll, Glencairn and Rothes, as well as other lairds. The Protestant nobles were annoyed that they had to ask Rizzio first before they could obtain an audience with Mary, and they also felt that as a Catholic he may have been working for Philip of Spain to encourage Mary to start a Catholic revolt.

The Queen may have been aware of the rumours that were spreading about herself and Rizzio, but she must have felt that her reputation had already withstood gossiping prior to her marriage and with her confinement fairly imminent there would be no reason for people to give them credence. Mary did not take into account that, although people may not believe malicious rumours, they can be used to other ends. Gradually those involved in the *Chaseabout Raid*, and others, drew Darnley and his father Lennox into their schemes.

Parliament was due to meet in March at which time the *Chaseabout* rebels were due to be charged with treason, and there were rumours that if Mary went ahead with this there would be trouble. The rumours were well known, even Elizabeth heard them, but although Mary considered pardoning the rebels, she changed her mind. She had been advised by her uncle the Cardinal of Lorraine to join with a league of leading continental Catholics. Although Mary did not agree to join the league, she announced that the meeting of parliament would go ahead – despite the possible threat from the rebels and their supporters.

The rebels had to act quickly, and therefore a bond was drawn and signed whereby it was to be ensured that the rebels would not be prosecuted. The actual wording was un-specific but Rizzio was to be got rid of by some means; and Darnley, in return for his support, would be guaranteed the crown matrimonial. Cunningly two of the signatories – Moray and Maitland – did not actually sign the bond even although they were most certainly involved.

On the evening of the 9 March 1566, two days after the session of parliament when it was decided that the rebels would be summoned on the 12 March, David Rizzio was murdered in front of the heavily pregnant Mary. She had been dining in her rooms at Holyrood Palace with her half-sister Jean, Countess of Argyll, her half-brother Robert Stewart and others of her household including Rizzio. Although it was Lent, because Mary was pregnant, she was excused from fasting, and just as the meal was served Darnley appeared from his apartments, accompanied by Patrick, third Lord

Ruthven, dressed in full armour. Ruthven was actually very ill at the time and looked extremely pale, and because he had a reputation for being interested in sorcery and the black arts, those in the room thought they were seeing a ghost. Ruthven, in reply to Mary's surprise, announced that he had come for Rizzio. Thereupon Rizzio attempted to hide – but to no avail.

Mary's attendants attempted to restrain Ruthven but as he pulled out a pistol the Earl of Morton's men burst into the room. Rizzio was stabbed as

The Murder of David Rizzio by Sir William Allan (1782–1850)

many as 56 times, and his body discarded over a chest – later his fine clothes were stolen by a porter. He is buried in Canongate cemetery, near Holyrood. Darnley's dagger was certainly used in the murder but it was used by his uncle, George Douglas, since – true to form – Darnley hung back during this fatal act.

Mary, once she recovered her wits, accused Darnley of betraying her, to which he replied that she had betrayed him with Rizzio. She was very angry, both for her secretary and for herself and her unborn child. When she retired for the night her thoughts were occupied with how much danger she was in, and how to make the best of this disaster. Indeed this latter thought probably weighed on the mind of her unreliable husband, as the next morning he came to her full of contrition. He was no doubt frightened by the situation, but once again Mary demonstrated her greater maturity by pointing out the political consequences of the murder. Darnley confessed the conspirators' plans to her, and it was then up to Mary to plan their escape. Whatever had happened, Darnley was the father of her child and to ensure its legitimacy she had to stand by him. Mary sent a message to the Earl of Bothwell via Lady Huntly – could he come to her aid?

Meantime the conspirators issued a proclamation, in Darnley's name, that the *Chaseabout* rebels had been pardoned. This left the way free for Moray to return without fear of prosecution, and he soon made his way to Holyrood Palace to call on his half-sister. The two siblings greeted each other with affection, but they were both playing a game of deceit. Moray had been one of the conspirators, but he made much show of being surprised at the news of the events of 9 March. On the other hand, if Darnley had told Mary the names of those involved in the plot then he would have had had no reason to omit Moray's name, so Mary probably knew of Moray's duplicity.

She managed to persuade Moray to allow her a midwife, even though she refused his request to pardon Rizzio's murderers. Of course the conspirators soon realized that Darnley was a weak link and they could not trust what he might say to Mary. They hoped that because it would be damaging to her reputation if it was revealed that the Queen's own husband had been involved in the murder, then she would agree to pardon them all. But Mary had other plans and played for time by saying that she was too ill to discuss the situation.

In the early hours of 12 March, only three days after Rizzio's murder, she and Darnley left Holyrood Palace by slipping out through back corridors and storerooms. Outside, her equerry, Arthur Erskine, had horses ready waiting for the couple. The journey through the night was not easy, especially for Mary in her advanced stage of pregnancy, and Darnley did not help matters by galloping ahead, fearful for his own life, with little concern for his wife and child. They eventually arrived at Dunbar Castle where Bothwell awaited them.

At Dunbar, Mary was joined by Huntly, Atholl, Fleming, Seton and Sir James Balfour and once Mary felt that she had enough support, she acted swiftly to finesse the conspirators. She offered to pardon those involved in the *Chaseabout*, separating them from Rizzio's murderers, who were not to be pardoned. When the rebels realized that they were outnumbered and outmanoeuvred, they quickly left the capital. Morton, Lindsay and Ruthven went south to England, Maitland went north and even the old war-horse Knox retreated to the west for safety. On her return to Edinburgh on 18 March, once again the conquering heroine, Mary accepted Moray, Glencairn and Argyll back into her council. For her personal safety, Mary moved into Edinburgh Castle where she awaited the birth of her baby; but Darnley, now that he felt the immediate danger had passed, returned to his life of

Edinburgh Castle

hedonism, and the relationship between Mary and her husband continued to deteriorate. The rumour-mongers started spreading stories that she would seek a divorce once the baby was born.

On the 3 June 1566 Mary made preparations for the birth; she was to be attended by her midwife Margaret Asteane and in keeping with her religious beliefs she sent for St Margaret of Scotland's relics, believing that these would provide her protection during the ordeal. Her labour pains started on 18 June and accounts state that she suffered greatly during the procedure, and some have even suggested that the Countess of Atholl tried to help by using sorcery.

Mary's son James was born on 19 June – a healthy baby born with the lucky caul (a piece of amniotic sac) over his head. According to folklore James could, at least, be assured he would not die by drowning. Mary summoned her husband to her chamber, to show him his son and assure him that no other was the father, which information Darnley greeted with his customary ill-humour. The news of a live birth, providing Scotland with a legitimate heir, may have been welcomed almost with ambivalence by his parents, but it was clearly a piece of news which Elizabeth received with even less pleasure. *The Queen of Scotland is lighter of a fair son and I am but barren stock* was her much quoted remark, and the arrival of James meant that he was not only heir to the Scottish throne, but also the English one.

The birth of the prince was met with much more spontaneous pleasure by the Scottish people, who were less concerned with the machinations of power and politics, and as the castle guns were fired in salute, hundreds of celebratory bonfires burned throughout the land and a service of thanksgiving was held at St Giles.

Mary may have enjoyed these first months of motherhood but her increasing dislike of her husband made time spent in his company little pleasure, and combined with a perhaps more than normal fear for her baby's life made the period after his birth quite stressful. Yet again Mary looked for a man on whom she could rely on for company and support, and this time it was the Earl of Bothwell who filled the role.

James Hepburn, Earl of Bothwell was 30 years old, and at least six inches shorter than Mary, but he was strong both physically and mentally – something Mary had not previously experienced in the men to whom she was attracted. Bothwell was also very successful in courting women, and although married he had many mistresses. Certainly physical attraction was probably not on Mary's mind when she appointed him lieutenant-general; it was his military strengths and political reliability which were more important. But attraction certainly came later and was to be one of Mary's greatest misjudgements.

In August Mary went on a hunting trip with Darnley to Traquair House, outside Peebles, but decided to send the young prince to Stirling Castle for safety, where he could be cared for by Earl of Mar, and in October she left Edinburgh on a progress through the borders holding justice ayres (peripatetic royal justice courts). She travelled to Jedburgh where she heard

Mary, Queen of Scots, and Darnley at Jedburgh, by Alfred Elmore (1877)

that Bothwell had received an injury during a skirmish with 'Wee' Jock Elliot, a border reiver. According to George Buchanan's account, which is critical of Mary, she immediately left Jedburgh to ride to Hermitage Castle to be at his side. However, as Mary herself was not feeling very well, it was actually five or six days before she made the journey. The 50-mile round trip by horse to Hermitage and back did bring on one of Mary's most serious bouts of illness. She had not been in good health since the birth and many, including herself, feared that she would die. It was at the tower house now called Queen Mary's House in Jedburgh, where she lay, virtually unconscious. She made it clear to those who attended her that Darnley was not to be allowed to take control of the crown.

On the 15 October, as Mary lay unconscious, her French surgeon Arnault attempted to revive her. He tightly bandaged her big toes, her legs from the ankles up and also her arms. He then forced wine into her mouth, gave her an enema and a medicinal draught, after which she vomited up a large amount of old blood. The symptoms appear to be those of a gastric or duodenal ulcer and she would have recurrent episodes of vomiting blood throughout her life.

As she recovered she was visited by Bothwell but not, alas, by her errant husband. She then continued north via Kelso, Hume Castle property of the Homes, then to Langton Castle owned by the Cockburns and Wedderburn another Home stronghold. Mary then stopped at Eyemouth, Dunbar and then Tantallon Castle just outside North Berwick which was at that time still a property of the Douglases. Before finally returning to Edinburgh, Mary stayed at Craigmillar Castle, Preston of Craigmillar's castle, and it was here that Mary and her advisors spent many hours in discussion about the problems posed by Darnley.

One option was to apply to Rome for an annulment but as Mary had already applied for permission to marry in the first place this was not feasible: this would also make her son illegitimate which she certainly did not want. Another possible solution was a divorce but this would make it impossible for her, as a Catholic, to remarry. A third suggestion, which Mary rejected, was that Darnley could be disposed of quickly and conveniently by other means. No decision was reached formally at this time, but it later became clear that Mary's council had decided on their course of action, which she may not have sanctioned officially.

The next important date on the calendar was the baptism of Prince James at Stirling on the 17 December. Darnley did not attend the ceremony, and in fact he and Mary spent hardly any time in each other's company for the rest of their married life. The baptism ceremony was planned to be a great celebration, reminiscent of the French festivals that Mary had experienced during her childhood. It would be a chance to relax and have pleasure after the strains of the last few months.

Prince James's godparents were to be the King of France, the Duke of Savoy and Elizabeth of England. Elizabeth did not attend but she sent a highly decorated gold christening font as a gift. The service was by Catholic rites, conducted by Archbishop Hamilton. The King of France's representative carried the baby to the Chapel Royal, accompanied by Scottish Catholic nobles. Elizabeth's representative, the Earl of Bedford, refused to enter the chapel as he was a Protestant, and he waited outside with other Protestant nobles including the Earls of Moray, Argyll and Bothwell. The ceremony was followed by a banquet in the Great Hall, then dancing and masques. The festivities lasted two days and culminated in a fireworks display. This celebration was also a symbolic demonstration of Mary's authority over her subjects, including any possibly rebellious nobles.

After the baptism, possibly again to show her authority, Mary granted the reformed church not only more of the benefices, but also a gift of £10 000. On the 24 December she pardoned Rizzio's murderers. By this time, Darnley had gone to Glasgow, probably suffering from secondary stage syphilis. Mary spent some days at Drummond Castle near Crieff accompanied by Bothwell.

Drummond Castle

In January 1567 she left for Glasgow to visit her sick husband, and they both then returned to Edinburgh.

Rumour has it that Mary was in fact pregnant again, but not by Darnley and therefore a reconciliation, if only for appearances, was important. The exact timing of Mary's second conception has always been unclear and open to speculation, and although she may not have been pregnant at this time, it seems likely that she did conceive sometime before her third marriage. Darnley was not very happy about returning with Mary as he felt that the conspirators would still blame him for his cowardice, but he finally agreed and they arrived in Edinburgh on 1 February. Mary did not want him to go to Holyrood as she did not want to risk any infection spreading to their child, no matter how unlikely. The only alternative accommodation was Kirk o' Field, a house near Holyrood Palace, which was owned by the Hamiltons.

During the time he spent at Kirk o' Field, meetings between himself and Mary were cordial and indeed Mary genuinely appeared to care for him. She agreed to sleep in the room below his because of his fears for his life, but relations between Darnley and Mary's nobles remained strained. As Darnley's health improved it was planned that he would move back to Holyrood on the 10 February but on the previous day, a Sunday, Darnley's future plans were prematurely halted.

There had been a celebration at the Palace that day for the marriage of one of Mary's pages, but the Queen had taken time away to spend with her husband. At about 10 o'clock she was reminded that she had promised to attend the masque so left Darnley and returned to the palace. At about two o'clock in the morning a large explosion disturbed the town and it was discovered that there was nothing but rubble – concealing several bodies – at the site of Kirk o' Field.

However the bodies under the rubble did not include Darnley, whose body, and that of his servant, was later discovered in the garden showing no signs of injuries caused by an explosion. Darnley and his servant appeared to have been suffocated. Darnley is buried in Holyrood Abbey. Mary was once more faced with a crisis of potentially enormous proportions, as on the one hand it might be shown that she had conspired in the murder, however it was carried out; but on the other hand there was always the possibility that Mary herself might have been in the house at the time and was therefore a possible target for assassination. How would she manage this crisis?

9 – Bothwell and battles

There have been many theories about Darnley's murder – from the motives behind it, to who was involved, how many plots there were and also how the assassination was carried out. It is likely that Bothwell was involved, as were others of Mary's nobles – Maitland, Morton and Moray, and that the discussions at Craigmillar were certainly associated with the plot. It is also

possible, as some have suggested, that it was hoped that the murder would be blamed on both Mary and Bothwell. The truth may always prove elusive, but it does seem that there may have been more than one group involved and

Earl of Bothwell by an unknown artist (1566)

more than one plan afoot that night. The outcome was still the same – Darnley was dead – and if Mary had previously thought it would be convenient to be rid of him, she was to be proved very wrong. Mary's actions from this time on were not those of an experienced and effective ruler, and she began to make some of her least successful and most ill-judged decisions.

Acting as custom demanded, Mary immediately went into mourning, but she did not remain in Edinburgh, instead she went to Seton Castle in East Lothian, home of Lord Seton. Prince James was left in the care of Huntly and Bothwell. During this time numerous placards appeared in Edinburgh linking her with Bothwell. The images on the placards were those of a hare surrounded by a circle of daggers, and of a mermaid wearing a crown. The meaning may be obscure to twentieth-century audiences but to sixteenth-century society the meaning was very clear – Bothwell's family crest included a hare and the swords implied he was a murderer; a mermaid commonly symbolised a prostitute but the addition of a crown left her identity in no doubt.

Mary came to Bothwell's defence and continued to consult him openly for advice, and she would not agree to a trial for the murder of her husband. It was Darnley's father, the Earl of Lennox who openly accused Bothwell of murder, and the privy council set the 12 April as the date for the trial. Bothwell managed to fill Edinburgh with his own supporters, so much so that Lennox was afraid to come to the city. The trial was held at the Tolbooth but, with Lennox absent, the prosecution had no witnesses or case, and so Bothwell was acquitted.

On the 19 April Mary attended parliament and formally took the reformed church under her protection. She also ratified gifts to Lethington, Morton, Moray, Lord Robert Stewart, Huntly and Bothwell. These actions may have been attempts to ensure support from the most powerful nobles in the country. Bothwell also organized his own personal support from bishops, earls and lords. The *Ainslie Tavern Bond* was an agreement to support Bothwell's claim to marry Mary and to provide him with armed support if need be. The bond had 29 signatories including Morton, Lethington, Argyll and Huntly, four of the most powerful men in Scotland apart from Bothwell. Again the ulterior motives for these actions are unclear – Bothwell may have had some powerful influence over them to persuade them that he was a suitable third husband or, in keeping with the duplicitous behaviour of the time, these nobles may have thought the plan would ruin both Mary and Bothwell. It must be said that Mary herself appears to have refused Bothwell's proposal several times, perhaps because she anticipated the consequences. Also before any wedding could be officially sanctioned, there was the minor detail of Bothwell's present wife.

Mary went to Stirling for a short visit to the young prince on 24 April and planned to return to Edinburgh via Linlithgow. It was here that Bothwell and his small army intercepted the royal party, which then travelled straight to Dunbar. Mary may have gone unwillingly or by choice, but by their return to Edinburgh on 6 May, after staying at Hailes Castle in East Lothian, a wedding was inevitable. Legend, and contemporary accounts by those present, suggest that it was here that Mary was raped by Bothwell, an action which forced Mary to agree to the wedding.

Once Bothwell's divorce was obtained on 7 May there were no further obstacles in the way. The plans may have shocked many, but there was little

Hailes Castle

obvious objection apart from the initial refusal by the Protestant minister of Edinburgh to proclaim their banns. The wedding contract was signed on 14 May and the ceremony took place the next day. There were several features which marked this day as very different from her previous two weddings. *Marry in May and rue the day* is a popular Scottish saying and for Mary this would turn out to be particularly apt. The wedding took place at 10 o'clock in the morning and the service was conducted according to Protestant rites. The rest of European royalty regarded Mary's conduct with surprise and shock but did, or could do, little to prevent it.

It did not take long for Mary to realize that this marriage was a serious misjudgement. Bothwell may have appeared a suitable husband for a short while, but the political repercussions of their union started very quickly. Bothwell's arrogance and lack of manners did little to ensure amicable relations with the rest of Mary's advisors. Even Mary discovered a less attractive side to him than previously, as he no longer appeared to give her the respect that as his Queen she was due. Public and private opinion turned against Bothwell, and despite the guarantees of the *Ainslie Tavern Bond* a group formed which pledged to free Mary from Bothwell's grip.

The couple had gone to Borthwick Castle in Midlothian after their wedding and the *Confederate Lords* assembled an army and marched from Stirling to meet the couple. Mary had few troops with her, so the couple had to slip out the castle quietly and head for Dunbar, where they hoped to

Borthwick Castle

organize their own troops. With the support of Huntly and Crawford, Mary raised an army and the two forces, of almost equal size, met at Carberry Hill near Musselburgh, near Edinburgh on 15 June. Bothwell, in his usual rash manner, was all for single combat, but Mary was against this. She also initially refused to agree to the offer that if she would desert Bothwell the lords would restore her to her rightful position.

As the day progressed the armies grew restless and less keen to attack their own countrymen, and many began to abandon their leaders. Mary, at length, agreed to return to Edinburgh if Bothwell was allowed to go free. She said her farewell to Bothwell and surrendered herself, to be brought in disgrace back to Edinburgh, where she was met not by cheering, welcoming crowds but by jeers and insults.

Instead of returning to Holyrood Palace, as she had thought, the lords took her to the Lord Provost's house, where she was kept under guard. From here the increasingly dishevelled Queen was taken to the Douglas castle on Lochleven, owned by Sir William Douglas, the Earl of Moray's half-brother. Mary had been told by the lords that they would not permit Bothwell to return to power. The Earl of Morton signed the warrant for Mary's imprisonment, where, although confined to the island, she was allowed to wander the grounds. She spent the first fortnight in a state of collapse – either because of pregnancy or general exhaustion.

It was at Lochleven that Mary finally agreed, on 24 July 1567, to abdicate in favour of her son. She had at first refused to sign or agree to a divorce from Bothwell, but the lords now had the added evidence of the highly questionable *Casket Letters*, love letters which suggested that Mary and

59

Bothwell had been having an affair before Darnley's death. The lords were anxious to get Mary to sign some agreement, otherwise their actions might be perceived as a rebellion against a rightful monarch. They also needed to establish a stable government to restore calm in the kingdom. If the Protestant lords did not establish a legal government quickly then Mary might obtain overseas help. As things stood Elizabeth, their most likely ally, rather than expressing pleasure at the problems of her rival, was extremely distressed that a legitimate monarch had been treated so badly.

Reports state that Mary had a miscarriage at Lochleven, some even that she lost twins. There has also been speculation about what stage the pregnancy had reached. There have also been questions about the date of conception, and whether or not Mary was pregnant in the January or as a result of the time spent at Dunbar. These questions will probably always remain unanswered, but she was certainly ill, miscarriage or not, in July. Her weakened state may have contributed to her acceptance of the terms offered. She agreed to resign her crown to her son because she could not carry out her duties as Queen and she agreed that Moray should be appointed Regent in James's minority but that Morton and the *Confederate Lords* would govern the country until he returned. James was crowned at Stirling Castle, where John Knox preached the sermon and Morton and Lord Home took the oath on James's behalf.

Bothwell in the meantime had, after he left Mary at Carberry, attempted to rally troops, but he found little support, even in the north-east stronghold of the Gordons. He then sailed to the northern isles of Orkney and Shetland, and raised a number of pirate ships to support him. When Kirkcaldy of Grange sailed north with armed ships, Bothwell made another hasty retreat to Norway, where he was eventually imprisoned. For a while King Frederick of Denmark held onto Bothwell in the hope that, in some way, he might be able to obtain the northern isles in return for his hostage, but by 1573 Bothwell was imprisoned at Dragsholm, where he went insane and died in 1578.

Back in Scotland Moray attempted to establish both political and religious control over the country. The religious acts of 1560 were ratified, much to the satisfaction of the General Assembly. Politically, Moray re-took Dunbar and Edinburgh, which had been held by the Queen's supporters, and restored peace in the border areas. Moray's Regency was not welcomed by all the nobles, especially the Hamiltons and George Gordon, the fifth Earl of Huntly, whose family title had been restored after forfeiture in 1562, and despite all Moray's efforts the country was not united. Mary still had a good amount of ground support which was inspired into action by her dramatic escape from captivity.

During her time on Lochleven, two young members of the Douglas family had become besotted by her and assisted her escape. They procured the keys of the castle, and late on 2 May 1568 Mary crept into a boat and was rowed to the shore where horses were waiting. She then met up with Lord Seton and rode to Niddry Castle near Winchburgh. From here she made her way west, to Cadzow Castle home of the Hamiltons, where she was pledged support by nine earls, nine bishops, 12 commendators and 18 lords – a mixture of Catholics and Protestants, and also some of those who had attended Moray's parliament. The support rapidly increased to 5000 or 6000 men and Mary and her party were optimistic of success.

Niddry Castle

Moray and his group – the King's party – had been caught off guard by her escape, and now was the time to strike. Moray was in Glasgow and Mary decided to march towards Dumbarton, near Glasgow, to try and attack before he got re-inforcements. On 13 May the two armies met at Langside, but despite having a smaller army, Moray's troops were more experienced and outmanoeuvred the Queen's troops. Mary initially tried to rally her troops, but there were personality clashes among her supporters as the Earl of Argyll, whom she had appointed commander, was not a popular choice.

As defeat became inevitable, she fled the battlefield, accompanied by Lord Herries, and made for Terregles Castle, a Maxwell property, and then Dundrennan Abbey where she called a meeting with her advisors – Herries, Fleming, Livingston, Boyd and George Douglas. She had decided to ask for help from Elizabeth, whom she felt, as a woman and monarch, would understand her position. Her advisors thought she should seek help from France – her own, and Scotland's, traditional ally. Mary could not be persuaded to change her mind, so a message was sent to Sir Richard

Lowther, deputy-governor of Carlisle, asking for safe passage for Mary and her party. Mary also wrote a personal letter to Elizabeth in which she explained her predicament, and without waiting for confirmation of her safe passage, on the 16 May disguised as an ordinary woman she crossed the River Solway and landed at Workington, spending her first night in England at Workington Hall, which was owned by a friend of Lord Herries.

Dundrennan Abbey

10 – Final years

Mary's arrival in England presented Elizabeth with something of a constitutional dilemma, but Mary had no idea of this when she arrived at Workington. Mary had never officially renounced her claim to the English crown, which annoyed Elizabeth, but Elizabeth could not be seen to support rebellion, and detaining Mary might be seen as tacit condonement of the action of the *Confederate Lords*.

Mary was escorted to Carlisle Castle, not straight to London as she had hoped. Nevertheless Mary accepted this, and did not realize that Elizabeth had instructed the Earl of Northumberland to guard her closely, and not only for her own protection. She also sent Sir Francis Knollys and Lord Scrope north as emissaries, not bearing an invitation south as Mary hoped, but to explain Elizabeth's position and her concerns about Darnley's murder. Mary was allowed a number of her own household to join her at Carlisle, but as time passed her impatience increased and she wrote numerous letters of complaint to Elizabeth and to France. Elizabeth would not have relished the prospect of Mary receiving French support, and so informed Mary that there would have to be an inquiry into

Bolton Castle

the events in Scotland. At the same time she moved Mary further south to Bolton Castle in Yorkshire. Mary sent some of her supporters back to

Scotland in the hope that they would be able to revive her position and popularity there. Although Mary continued to have support throughout her captivity, it was an ever decreasing force and had lost momentum, and its figurehead, when she fled south.

At Bolton, although aware she was to all intents a prisoner, Mary did receive occasionally hopeful items of news. Moray was not a popular Regent and Huntly and Argyll still hoped to overthrow him. The Cardinal of Lorraine and Charles IX of France assured her of support, which was in the event to prove more theoretical than real.

Mary was offered the opportunity to have her case heard by Elizabeth – if she would renounce her claim to the English crown, to which Mary agreed. She also agreed to Elizabeth's condition that she break off communications and alliances with France; and finally she was to forbid the celebration of the Mass in Scotland, although Mary herself would be permitted to worship in private as her faith dictated.

Mary agreed to all these conditions, believing that she would be proved innocent of all charges, but this illusion was shattered when she was informed of two unsettling facts. Firstly she was not to be allowed to attend the inquiry herself, and secondly Moray and Morton had sent south the infamous *Casket Letters*, which purported to contain love letters between Mary and Bothwell, showing that they were lovers before Darnley was killed.

These letters disappeared soon after the York inquiry, but their authenticity has always been doubtful, especially as those who discovered (or doctored) them had so much to gain from anything that blackened Mary's name. Thus Morton and his able assistant, George Buchanan, whose blatant allegiance to Morton and use of anti-Mary/anti-Hamilton propaganda, make his evidence suspect, used the letters to add weight to their case. Whether or not the letters were complete fakes or were merely doctored a little, is now of little importance, as they were not even produced at York. In the end Elizabeth decided that neither side had proved their case adequately, but Mary's reputation was sufficiently sullied to justify keeping her captive. The casket which was supposed to have held the letters is now kept at Lennoxlove House in East Lothian.

Meanwhile back in Scotland, Mary's cause was not entirely lost and would not be until 1573; several of her nobles never joined the King's party, particularly Huntly and Châtelherault. The two parties did not divide simply along religious lines; although the King's party supported the reformed church, there were both Catholics and Protestants on Mary's side.

Often the divide occurred along political and old dynastic rivalries. As Regent Moray had not consolidated his powerbase, therefore his assassination at Linlithgow on 23 January 1570, organized by the Hamiltons, was not unexpected. Lennox, Darnley's father, was appointed Regent next, but his agenda of revenge against Darnley's murderers did not make him a more popular choice. The north-east was held for Mary by Huntly, the west by the Hamiltons and Edinburgh Castle by Kirkcaldy of Grange and Maitland. Despite the Queen's party holding a parliament in the Tolbooth in Edinburgh in June 1571, the rival party increased its support as more of the nobles changed their allegiance.

The King's party was tightly controlled by the Earl of Morton, James Douglas, although he was not officially appointed regent until 1572. With English help, Morton attacked Edinburgh Castle, and on its fall Kirkcaldy of Grange was hanged. Maitland was saved this fate by dying, possibly by poison, before being captured. In 1571 Archbishop John Hamilton – who was on Mary's side – was captured, and later hanged, during the seizure of Dumbarton Castle by the King's troops. Châtelherault and Huntly agreed to peace terms at Perth in 1573, and over the next three years Argyll (1574), Châtelherault (1575) and Huntly (1576) all died, leaving the governing of the country to Morton, who managed to impose a period of relative tranquillity on the country.

Morton's personality and style of government did not mean that he did not have any problems or create enemies. Old feuds lingered, and combined with Morton's disastrous financial and pro-English policies, contributed to his own overthrow as Regent in 1578. He was eventually arrested, and executed in 1580 for his part in the murder of Darnley. Aberdour Castle in Fife was one of the Earl of Morton's castles.

Aberdour Castle

Mary, in England, had her own problems. She was moved to Tutbury Castle in 1569, and to several other locations over the next few years. Her captors and conditions were as varied as the locations; sometimes more friendly, at others distant and rigid. She was allowed to have some of her own household with her during her captivity, and she was allowed visitors and communications from outside, but she did not have freedom to come and go as she wished, and spies reported on her movements and communications. Her health also deteriorated during her imprisonment, a deterioration possibly contributed to by the damp conditions of some of the accommodation and by a lack of regular exercise. There are reports of a rheumatic-like condition, associated with fever, for which she visited the thermal baths at Buxton Wells on several occasions. In the 1580s she had several episodes of dropsy, when her legs became swollen and weak, and throughout the latter years of her life Mary required frequent visits and treatments from a number of physicians.

Mary was still, as she had been throughout her life, an enigma and a fascination to many men. She was not above using her power and influence over them to manipulate and attempt to alter her circumstances, and there were several episodes of plotting and attempts at escape during her years of confinement. One episode, in 1571, involved the Duke of Norfolk and included a proposal for a marriage between himself and Mary. Messages were sent to Rome asking for an annulment from Bothwell, who was still alive although in prison. The episode is also known as the *Ridolfi Plot*, as Spanish support was also expected to help raise the Catholics in England.

The plot was discovered and Elizabeth had Norfolk imprisoned in the Tower of London and later executed. Another marriage plan was instigated by the Pope, who suggested Philip II's half-brother Don John of Austria, but he died of typhus. Events outwith England also contributed to Mary's precarious popularity; on the 24 August 1572, on the eve of the Feast of St Bartholomew, thousands of Protestants were slaughtered in Paris. As a result there was an increase of anti-Catholic feeling throughout Europe and in England with reminiscences of the brutalities of Mary Tudor's reign, and distrust of Mary Stewart increased, especially as rumours about her plotting spread.

Elizabeth, in contrast, actually became a little more lenient to Mary at this time, and allowed her to be moved to Chatsworth Hall because her health had deteriorated, and over the next years she spent her captivity at Buxton, Chatsworth and Sheffield. With fear of Catholic plots abounding, Elizabeth appointed Sir Francis Walsingham to root out any treasonable plans. He was a stern Protestant and determined to use whatever means necessary to rid Elizabeth of Catholic dangers, especially Mary.

Walsingham enrolled the services of a former Catholic priest Gilbert Gifford, who then asked for an audience with Mary. He told her that he was in touch with her continental friends and offered to smuggle letters out to them. Mary was by this time held at Chartley Hall and had suffered quite a serious bout of illness. She may have been physically and emotionally vulnerable and so less cautious. In 1586, a local brewer appeared, organized by Gilbert Gifford, bearing a secret letter from her supporters on the continent. Mary dictated a reply to her French secretary, Claud Nau, who translated them into code and gave them to the brewer to pass on. The letters did not go straight to their intended destination, but were instead re-routed via Walsingham who, from now on, was privy to all Mary's communications.

In June 1586 Mary was in touch with the leader of a group of Catholics, Sir Anthony Babington, who wrote describing details of his plan to assassinate Elizabeth and place Mary on the throne. Mary was aware that if she approved of his plan, and it was a failure, then she would suffer serious consequences. She was advised not to reply to Babington, but at the same time her alternative hopes for a return to Scotland had been abruptly interrupted.

Mary's son James was now twenty, and although she had written him affectionate letters there was probably never a real closeness between them. James had been brought up as a Protestant and taught to distrust his mother by his tutor George Buchanan. In the summer of 1586 he had signed an Anglo-Scottish agreement, whereby Elizabeth would name James as her successor and grant him a pension, in return for peace between the two countries.

Mary was very disappointed when she heard this news, and it may have contributed to her rashness in conveying her approval to Babington, which information was in turn, of course, received by Walsingham and Elizabeth. On 11 August Mary was allowed to go out on a hunt, much to her surprise; but during the day she was confronted with the news that Elizabeth knew of the plot. Her rooms had been searched for evidence, and her servants arrested – they later confessed. Babington had been tried and executed in London. Mary's last attempt at freedom had failed and she was removed to Fotheringhay Castle on the 24 September 1586, where she was to stand trial for her part in a plot to destroy Elizabeth.

The trial started on 15 October and evidence of the *Babington Plot* was produced in the form of copies of Mary's correspondence. Mary, who wore black velvet as had become her custom, was suffering badly from rheumatism and had difficulty walking unaided, but she maintained her dignity throughout the proceedings, and answered the accusations as best she could without the benefit of legal advice or witnesses on her behalf. She admitted to the court that she had become tired of her confinement, and had wished for escape, that she had written to Catholics on the continent and that her faith was important to her; but she denied that she had conspired to bring about the death of Elizabeth.

On 25 October Elizabeth's courtiers announced their verdict – Mary was found guilty. Throughout the winter of 1586 and into 1587 Mary awaited Elizabeth's formal signing of her death warrant, which Elizabeth was somewhat reluctant to do in case there would be repercussions against her. She finally signed it on 1 February 1587, and when the news was conveyed to Mary, she expressed her relief that she would be finally free of a life which had become so miserable.

Mary spent her last night with her servants, praying and writing, and at six o'clock she dressed in a black satin gown over a red velvet petticoat, with a long fine white veil which reached to her feet and a white cap on her head.

The Execution of Mary, Queen of Scots by Robert Herdman (1867)

She put on a gold rosary and was accompanied by six of her servants into the Great Hall at Fotheringhay where a platform had been erected. The death warrant was read out and Mary prayed aloud in Latin and English, the executioner Bulle asked her forgiveness as was customary. Covering her eyes with a gold-fringed cloth she laid her head upon the block. Mary's last words were *Into thy hands, O Lord, I commend my spirit*. It then took two blows of the axe to sever Mary's head and so end the life of one of Scotland's, and Europe's, most enigmatic monarchs.

Epilogue – King James VI and I

James VI, son of Mary and Darnley, acceded to the English throne in 1603, so uniting the crowns of Scots and England, although the two kingdoms retained separate parliaments until 1707.

In 1612 James VI had his mother's body brought from Peterborough Cathedral and re-buried in Westminster Abbey. He later ordered the demolition of Fotheringhay Castle, the place where Mary had been executed.

Places in Scotland to Visit

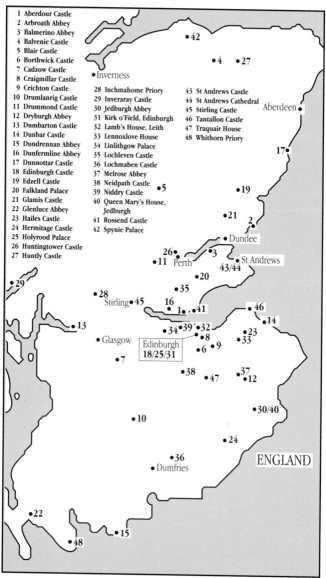

1 Aberdour Castle
2 Arbroath Abbey
3 Balmerino Abbey
4 Balvenie Castle
5 Blair Castle
6 Borthwick Castle
7 Cadzow Castle
8 Craigmillar Castle
9 Crichton Castle
10 Drumlanrig Castle
11 Drummond Castle
12 Dryburgh Abbey
13 Dumbarton Castle
14 Dunbar Castle
15 Dundrennan Abbey
16 Dunfermline Abbey
17 Dunnottar Castle
18 Edinburgh Castle
19 Edzell Castle
20 Falkland Palace
21 Glamis Castle
22 Glenluce Abbey
23 Hailes Castle
24 Hermitage Castle
25 Holyrood Palace
26 Huntingtower Castle
27 Huntly Castle

28 Inchmahome Priory
29 Inveraray Castle
30 Jedburgh Abbey
31 Kirk o'Field, Edinburgh
32 Lamb's House, Leith
33 Lennoxlove House
34 Linlithgow Palace
35 Lochleven Castle
36 Lochmaben Castle
37 Melrose Abbey
38 Neidpath Castle
39 Niddry Castle
40 Queen Mary's House, Jedburgh
41 Rossend Castle
42 Spynie Palace

43 St Andrews Castle
44 St Andrews Cathedral
45 Stirling Castle
46 Tantallon Castle
47 Traquair House
48 Whithorn Priory

Places to Visit in Scotland

P	Parking
S	Sales Area
☕	Refreshments
wc	Toilet
£	Admission Charge
&	Disabled
HS	Historic Scotland
NTS	National Trust for Scot.
EH	English Heritage

1 Aberdour Castle

NT 193854 66 HS

On A921, Aberdour, Fife

Large ruined castle, dating from the 14th century, home of the Douglases. Once home of James Douglas, Regent Morton, who was executed in 1581. Terraced garden.

📞 01383 860519—Open all year except closed Thur PM and Fri October to March

P **☕** **S** **wc** **£** **&** **wc**

2 Arbroath Abbey

NO 643413 54 HS

Off A92, in Arbroath, Angus

Substantial ruins of a Tironensian abbey, founded in 1178 by William the Lyon to commemorate the death of his friend, Thomas à Becket. *The Declaration of Arbroath*, asserting Scotland's independence from English rule, was signed here in 1320.

Mary visited here in 1562 during a progress, staying at the Abbot's House. Museum.

📞 01241 878756—Open all year

P Nearby **S** **£**

3 Balmerino Abbey

NO 358246 59 NTS

Off A914, 4.5 miles SW of Newport on Tay, Fife

Remains of a 13th-century Cistercian Abbey in a peaceful setting, founded by Ermengarde, widow of William the Lyon, and Alexander II, in 1229. The basement of the chapter house and adjoining buildings survive. Interesting tree.

Mary had dinner at the Abbey during a progress in 1565, although it had been sacked by Reformers in 1547 and 1559.

Open all year

4 Balvenie Castle

NJ 326409 28 HS

On B975, 0.5 miles N of Dufftown

Large ruined castle, with a 13th-century curtain wall enclosing ranges of buildings. Held by the Comyns, Douglases, Stewarts, Innes family, and the Duffs.

Mary probably stayed at the castle in 1562 when it was a property of John Stewart, Earl of Atholl.

📞 01340 820121—Open April to September

P **S** **£**

5 Blair Castle

NN 867662 43

Off B8079, 1 mile NW of Blair Atholl, Perthshire

Blair Castle, dating from the 13th century, is a large castle and mansion, home of the Dukes of Atholl for nearly 800 years.

Mary stayed here in 1564.

Many rooms. Collections of paintings, arms, armour, china, costumes and Jacobite mementoes. Garden and park.

☎ 01796 481207—Open April to October

P ▬ S WC ♿ Lim access

6 Borthwick Castle

NT 370597 66

Off A7, 2 miles SE of Gorebridge, Midlothian

One of the best-preserved castles in Scotland, the castle consists of a massive U-plan keep and was built by the Borthwick family in the 15th century. The castle was bombarded by Cromwell in 1650.

Mary visited here in 1563 during a progress, and again after marrying Bothwell in 1567. She was besieged at the castle, and had to escape disguised as a page-boy.

☎ 01875 820514– Hotel – open mid-March to January 2 and to non-residents

P ▬ WC

Borthwick Castle

7 Cadzow Castle

NS 734538 64

Off A72, 1.5 miles SE of Hamilton, Lanarkshire

A very ruined castle of the Hamiltons, the 2nd Earl was made Duke of Châtelherault in the 16th century. The castle was started in the 12th century, but mostly consists of a later tower house.

Mary came here after escaping from Lochleven Castle in 1568, and the castle was besieged in 1570 and again in 1579, when it was dismantled.

View from exterior as dangerously ruined.

☎ 01698 426213—In Châtelherault

Country Park. Open all year except Christmas and New Year

8 Craigmillar Castle
NT 288709 66 HS
Off A6095 or A68, 3 miles SE of centre of Edinburgh
An imposing ruin, Craigmillar Castle consists of a 14th-century keep surrounded by courtyards. The existing castle was mostly built by the Preston family.

Mary stayed here in 1566 after the slaying of Rizzio, and it was at Craigmillar that the plot to murder Darnley was hatched. Visitor centre.
☎ 0131 661 4445—Open all year except closed Thur PM and Fri October to March

P S &

9 Crichton Castle
NT 380612 66 HS
Off B6367, 2 miles E of Gorebridge, Midlothian
Fine ruined courtyard castle, with a diamond-fashioned facade, consisting of a 14th-century keep and later ranges of buildings. It was built by the Crichtons, but was later held by the Hepburn Earls of Bothwell.

It was at the castle that Mary attended the wedding of her half-brother Lord James Stewart to Lady Janet Hepburn in 1562.
☎ 01875 320017—Open April to September – 600 yard walk to castle

 P S &

10 Drumlanrig Castle
NX 851992 78
Off A76, 3 miles N of Thornhill, Dumfriesshire
A magnificent 17th-century courtyard mansion, built for the Douglas family, which stands on the site of a 15th-century castle.

Mary visited the old castle in 1563 during a progress.

Renowned art collection, including works by Rembrandt, Leonardo and Holbein. Gardens. Visitor centre.
☎ 01848 330248—Open early May to late August except Thur

P 🍴 S WC & Access

11 Drummond Castle
NN 844181 58
Off A822, 2.5 miles SW of Crieff, Perthshire
An impressive 15th-century castle, which has been extended and enlarged in later centuries. It was built by the Drummond family.

Mary stayed here with Bothwell 1566-7 after the baptism of Prince James, later James VI.

Magnificent formal garden.
☎ 01764 681321—Castle not open. Gardens open Easter; open May to October.

P &

12 Dryburgh Abbey
NT 591316 74 HS
Off B6356, Dryburgh, 5 miles SE of Melrose, Borders
A picturesque and substantial ruin, Dryburgh Abbey dates from the 12th and 13th centuries, and is where Sir

Dryburgh Abbey

Walter Scott is buried. It was founded by David I.

The Abbey was sacked by the English 1544-45 during the *Rough Wooing*.

☎ 01835 822381—Open all year

🅿️ 🆂 🚾 ♿

13 Dumbarton Castle

NS 400745 64 HS

Off A814, Dumbarton

Dumbarton was a formidable fortress from before the 5th century until the 17th century.

Mary was kept here for safety until leaving for France in 1548. She visited again in 1563 during a progress, and the castle was held for her captured by the King's Party in 1571.

☎ 01389 732167—Open all year except closed Thur PM and Fri October to March

🅿️ 🆂 🚾 ♿

14 Dunbar Castle

NT 678794 67

Off A1087, nr harbour, Dunbar, East Lothian

Once one of the most important castles in Scotland, very little remains of Dunbar Castle. It was a Royal castle,

was besieged often, but was finally destroyed in the 19th century to build a harbour.

The castle was sacked in 1548, but was garrisoned by the French in the 1550s. Mary and Darnley stayed here in 1566, and Mary was also brought to the castle in 1567 after being *abducted* by Bothwell.

Open all year

🅿️ Nearby

15 Dundrennan Abbey

NX 749475 83 HS

On A711, Dundrennan, 5 miles SE of Kirkcudbright, Dumfries and Galloway

The picturesque ruins of a Cistercian abbey founded in 1142 by David I.

Mary spent her last night here (15/16 May) on Scottish soil before fleeing to England in 1568.

☎ 01557 500262—Open April to September

🅿️ 🆂 ♿

16 Dunfermline Abbey

NT 089873 65 HS

Off A907 or A823, in Dunfermline, Fife

Site of 11th-century Benedictine monastery, founded by Queen Margaret, wife of Malcolm Canmore. The restored church dates from the 12th century, and there are ruins of the domestic buildings as well as the 16th-century palace, remodelled from the guest house of the abbey. Robert the Bruce is buried in the church.

Mary stayed in the palace here in 1565. Exhibition.

📞 01383 739026—Choir of church closed October to March

🅿 Nearby S &

17 Dunnottar Castle

NO 882839 45

Off A92, 2 miles S of Stonehaven, Aberdeenshire

In a spectacular location, Dunnottar Castle is a formidable stronghold, built on a promontory, with a keep, ranges of buildings and fortified entrance. It was held by the Keith Earl Marischals.

Mary stayed here in 1562 during a progress.

Climb to castle, and back.

📞 01569 762173—Open all year except weekends in winter, 25/26 December & 1/2 January

🅿 &

18 Edinburgh Castle

NT 252735 66 HS

Edinburgh

One of the strongest and most important castles in Scotland, Edinburgh Castle covers a large area and was a fortress from earliest times, although most of the buildings are 16th century or later. The Scottish Crown Jewels are kept here, as is the huge 15th-century cannon, Mons Meg. St Margaret's Chapel, dedicated to Queen Margaret, wife of Malcolm Canmore, dates from the 12th century. The Stone of Destiny is to be displayed at the castle from 30 November 1996.

Mary of Guise died here in 1560, and Mary gave birth to Prince James, later James VI, in 1566. Mary made a procession from here down the Royal Mile to Holyrood Palace in 1561.

📞 0131 225 9846—Open all year; courtesy vehicle can take visitors with disabilities to Crown Square

🅿 ☕ S WC & & WC/Facilities

19 Edzell Castle

NO 585693 44 HS

Off B966, 6 miles N of Brechin, Angus

Home of the Lindsay Earls of Crawford from 1357 until about 1764, the castle consists of a ruined tower house at one corner of a large courtyard with ranges of buildings.

Mary stayed here in 1562 during a progress.

Large and fine walled garden. Visitor centre.

📞 01356 648631—Open all year except closed Thur PM and Fri October to March

🅿 S WC & & WC/Lim acc

20 Falkland Palace

NO 254075 59 NTS

On A912, 4 miles N of Glenrothes, Fife

A fortified but comfortable residence of the Kings of Scots, the gatehouse block of Falkland Palace is complete, while other ranges are ruined. It was used by James III, James IV and James V, who died here in 1542. Mary stayed here in 1563 and 1565.

Garden. Visitor centre. Exhibition.

📞 01337 857397—Open April to October

🅿 Nearby S WC & & Facilities

21 Glamis Castle
NO 387481 54
Off A928, 6 miles W of Forfar, Angus
Glamis Castle is a magnificent 14th-century keep, modified and greatly extended in later times. It is the home of the Lyon family, Earls of Strathmore and Kinghorne, and houses many treasures.

Mary stayed at the castle in 1562 during a progress.

✆ 01307 840393—Open April to October

22 Glenluce Abbey
NX 185586 82 HS
Off A75, 1.5 miles N of Glenluce village, Dumfries and Galloway
Ruins of a Cistercian abbey dating from 1192 in a pleasant location, the chapter house of which is still roofed.

Mary stayed here in 1563 during a progress.

Exhibition.

✆ 01581 300541—Open daily April to September; weekends only October to March

P S £

23 Hailes Castle
NT 575758 67 HS
Off A1, 1.5 miles SW of East Linton, East Lothian
Hailes Castle is a picturesque ruined castle, mostly dating from the 14th to 16th centuries. It was held by the Hepburns, but was partly dismantled by Cromwell in 1650.

Mary and Bothwell stayed here in 1567 on their way from Dunbar to Edinburgh after Bothwell had *abducted* her.

✆ 0131 668 8800—Open all year

P

24 Hermitage Castle
NY 497960 79 HS
Off B6399, 5 miles N of Newcastleton, Borders
A forbidding Border stronghold, Hermitage Castle is a large ruined courtyard castle, dating mostly from the 13th and 14th centuries. It was held by the Douglases, but in 1492 was sold to the Hepburns.

Mary visited Bothwell here after he had been badly wounded in a fight with the Elliots. She returned to Jedburgh, where she stayed at Queen Mary's House, but made herself ill from the long ride.

✆ 01387 376222—Open daily April to September

25 Holyrood Palace
NT 269739 66 HS
1 mile E of Edinburgh Castle
This fine and interesting palace, one range of which dates from the 16th century, is the official residence of the monarch in Scotland.

Mary attended a Mass in the nearby Abbey church in 1561, and she was married to Darnley at the chapel in 1565. David Rizzio, favourite of Mary, was murdered here in front of her by Darnley and others in 1566, *blood* marking the spot where his body lay. The palace houses a collection of pictures and mementoes associated with Mary.

The ruins of the Abbey church adjoin the palace, in which Darnley is buried, while Rizzio is buried at the nearby Canongate cemetery.

☏ 0131 556 1096—Open all year except during Queen's residence

 Nearby S ♿

26 Huntingtower Castle

NO 083252 58 HS

On A85, 2.5 miles NW of Perth

The oldest part of the splendid castle of Huntingtower is a 15th-century keep, to which was added a 16th-century tower house, and later a joining block, all still roofed. It was originally held by the Ruthven family, and has early wall paintings.

Mary visited the castle with Darnley in 1565 while on their honeymoon.

☏ 01738 627231—Open all year except Thur PM and Fri October to March

P S ♿

27 Huntly Castle

NJ 532407 29 HS

Off A920, Huntly, Aberdeenshire

A fine building with a long and turbulent history, the substantial ruins of Huntly Castle date mostly from the 15th and 16th centuries. It was the main seat of the Gordon Earls of Huntly.

The castle was sacked by Mary's forces after they had defeated the Gordons at the battle of Corrichie in 1562.

☏ 01466 793191—Open all year except Thur PM and Fri October to March

P S WC ♿

28 Inchmahome Priory

NN 574005 57 HS

Off A81, island in the Lake of Menteith, Stirlingshire

Picturesque ruins of a small Augustinian priory, founded in 1238 by Walter Comyn, Earl of Menteith on a pleasant

Huntingtower Castle

island in a loch.

Mary was kept at the Priory for safety in 1547, before being moved to Dumbarton Castle, and then France in 1548.

📞 01877 385294—Open April to September – ferry from Port of Menteith.

P S WC ⅃

29 Inveraray Castle

NN 096093 56
Off A819 or A83, to N of Inveraray, Argyll

Inveraray Castle, begun in 1743, is a fine large symmetrical mansion, built for the Campbell Dukes of Argyll. An older castle, which has been demolished, stood nearby

Mary stayed at the old castle on a progress in 1563.

Collections of weaponry, tapestries and furniture. Garden.

📞 01499 302203—Open April to June & September to mid-October Sat to Thur; July & August daily

P ⬤ S WC ⅃

⅃ Limited access

30 Jedburgh Abbey

NT 650204 74 HS
Off A68, Jedburgh, Borders

Founded by David I about 1138 as an Augustinian abbey, much of the fine church and some foundations of the domestic

buildings survive.

The Abbey was sacked during the *Rough Wooing* in 1544-5.

Visitor centre.

📞 01835 863925—Open all year

P ⬤ S WC ⅃ ♿ WC/Lim acc

31 Kirk o' Field, Edinburgh

NT 260735 66
Old College, University of Edinburgh, Edinburgh

Site of the house where Darnley and his servant were suffocated in 1567 after the building had been blown up with gunpowder.

Site only

Jedburgh Abbey

32 Lamb's House, Leith
NT 269764   66
*Leith, 2 miles NE of Edinburgh
Castle*
The house of Lamb, a Leith merchant.
Mary and rested here on arrival from
France in 1561. The house is now an
old people's day centre.
View from outside only

33 Lennoxlove House
NT 515721   66
*Off B6369 and B6368, 1 mile S of
Haddington, East Lothian*
Dating from the 15th century or
before, Lennoxlove House incorpo-
rates a tower house into the later
splendid mansion. Treasures include
the death mask of Mary, Queen of
Scots, and casket from the *Casket
Letters*, as well as collections of
portraits, furniture and porcelain.
  Lennoxlove, or Lethington as it was
once known, was a property of Sir
Richard Maitland of Lethington, who
died – and may have been poisoned –
after the capture of Edinburgh Castle
in 1573.
☎ 01620 823720—Open Easter to
October, Wed, Thu, Sat and Sun:
telephone to confirm.
P ☕ **WC** ⅋ ♿ **WC**/Gardens

34 Linlithgow Palace
NT 003774   65 HS
Off A803, Linlithgow, West Lothian
Once a magnificent palace and still a
spectacular ruin, Linlithgow Palace
consists of a courtyard surrounded by
ranges of buildings. It was used by the
Stewart kings, and James V was born
here in 1512, as was Mary was in 1542.
Mary visited the palace during a

progress in 1564, and it was from near
here that she was *abducted* by
Bothwell in 1567. Museum.
  Near the Palace is the *Linlithgow
Story*, a museum recounting the story
of the town, including the visits of
Mary.
☎ 01506 842896—Open all year
P **S** **WC** Nearby ⅋

35 Lochleven Castle
NO 138018   58 HS
*Off B996, 1 mile E of Kinross,
Perthshire*
Standing on a small island in Loch
Leven, the picturesque castle consists
of a 15th-century keep with a small
courtyard.
  Mary was imprisoned here in 1567-8,
during which time she signed her
abdication, although she later escaped.
☎ 01786 450000—Open April to
September; ferry out to island
from Kinross
P **S** **WC** ⅋ ♿ **WC**

36 Lochmaben Castle
NY 088812   78 HS
*Off B7020, 0.5 miles S of Lochma-
ben, Dumfriesshire*
One a strong fortress, little remains of
a Bruce castle, which dates from as
early as the 13th century.
  James V made Lochmaben his base
before his forces were defeated at the
battle of Solway Moss in 1542. Mary
and Darnley attended a banquet here
in 1566 during the *Chaseabout Raid*.
Open all year – view from exterior
P

37 Melrose Abbey

NT 548341 73 HS
Off A6091, Melrose, Borders

An elegant and picturesque ruin,
Melrose Abbey was founded by David I
about 1136 as a Cistercian abbey. The
heart of Robert the Bruce was buried
here, as are many of the Douglas
family.

The Abbey was sacked by the English
during the *Rough Wooing* in 1544-5,
when the Douglas tombs were
desecrated. Museum.

☎ 01896 822562

Open all year

P S WC ⅋

38 Neidpath Castle

NT 236405 73
*On A72, 1 mile W of
Peebles, Borders*

Standing on a steep bank
of a river, Neidpath Castle
is an imposing 14th-
century keep with a small
courtyard. It has been
home to the Frasers, Hays,
Douglases and Wemyss
families, and was besieged
by Cromwell in 1650.

Mary stayed at the castle
in 1563, as did her son,
James VI,
in 1587. Museum.

☎ 01721 720333—
Telephone to confirm
opening days and times

P S ⅋

♿ Grnd flr/Museum

39 Niddry Castle

NT 097743 65
*Off A89, 2 miles NE of Broxburn,
West Lothian*

Niddry Castle is a restored four-storey
L-plan castle. It dates from the 15th
century, and a property of the Setons.

It was here that Mary came after
escaping from Lochleven Castle in
1568.

View from outside

Neidpath Castle

40 Queen Mary's House, Jedburgh

NT 651206 74

Off A68, Jedburgh, nr Abbey, Borders

Queen Mary's House is a T-plan 16th-century tower house, and was where Mary stayed in 1566. During her visit she made the long ride to Hermitage Castle to see Bothwell, who had been wounded. When Mary returned to Jedburgh, she was seriously ill herself for several days.

Museum with displays about Mary's visit to Jedburgh

☏ 01835 863331—Open March to November

P Nearby S WC

41 Rossend Castle

NT 225859 66

Off A921, overlooking harbour, Burntisland, Fife

Standing on a hill above the harbour, Rossend Castle is a restored E-plan tower house, dating from the 16th century. It was held by the Durie family, and then the Melvilles.

Mary was attacked here by the poet Châtelard in 1563, a crime for which he was executed at St Andrews.

View from outside.

42 Spynie Palace

NJ 231658 28 HS

Off A941, 2.5 miles N of Elgin, Moray

Built by the Bishops of Elgin, the impressive ruins of Spynie Palace consist of a massive 15th-century keep and courtyard, with towers at the corners.

Mary visited the Palace in 1562 during a progress. Bothwell fled here after the battle of Carberry Hill in 1567.

☏ 01343 546358—Open daily in summer; weekends only in winter – joint ticket with Elgin Cathedral

P S WC   varphi ♿ WC

43 St Andrews Castle

NO 513169 59 HS

Off A91, St Andrews, Fife

Close to the Cathedral, the castle is a very ruinous courtyard castle, with the remains of the gatehouse and other towers. Cardinal Beaton was murdered here in 1546, his naked body hung from one of the windows, and there are the remains of a mine and counter-mine from the resultant siege of the castle.

Visitor centre. Exhibition.

☏ 01334 477196—Open all year; ticket available for castle and cathedral

P Nearby S WC varphi ♿ WC

Spynie Palace

83

Traquair House (see next page)

44 St Andrews Cathedral
NO 516166 59 HS
Off A91, St Andrews, Fife
The very ruined remains of the largest
cathedral in Scotland, with St Rule's
Tower. Museum houses a fine
collection of early Christian and
medieval sculpture.

It was in the town that the Protestant
martyr George Wishart was burnt by
Cardinal Beaton in 1546, and the
French poet Châtelard was also
executed after attacking Mary at
Rossend in 1563.

☎ 01334 472563—Open all year –
combined ticket available for
Cathedral and Castle.

P Nearby S &

45 Stirling Castle
NS 790940 57 HS
Stirling
One of the most important, powerful
and well-preserved castles in Scotland,
Stirling Castle is a courtyard castle with
ranges of buildings, including a palace

built by the Stewart monarchs. It was
besieged by Edward I in 1304.

Mary was brought here for safety and
crowned in the chapel in 1543, and
later visited frequently. The future
James VI was baptised in the Chapel
Royal in 1566, and was crowned king
here in 1567 after Mary's abdication.
Visitor centre. Exhibitions. Garden.

☎ 01786 450000—Open all year

P ☕ S WC £ & WC/Access

46 Tantallon Castle
NT 596851 67 HS
*On A198, 3 miles E of North
Berwick, East Lothian*
A massive and impressive ruin,
Tantallon Castle has a huge wall of
stone, a gatehouse and corner towers,
and was held by the Douglases.

Mary stayed here in 1566 during a
progress on her way to Craigmillar.

☎ 01620 892727—Open all year
except closed Thur PM and Fri
October to March

P ☕ S WC £

47 Traquair House
NT 330354 73
*On B709,1 mile S of Innerleithen,
Borders*
Reputedly one of the oldest continuously occupied houses in Scotland, Traquair is a complex building, dating from as early as the 12th century.

Mary stayed here in 1566 while on a hunting trip with Lord Darnley, and Traquair houses mementoes associated with her, as well as with Bonnie Prince Charlie and the Jacobites.

1745 Cottage Restaurant. Working 18th-century brewery. Garden & maze. Craft workshops.

☎ 01896 830323—Open daily Easter to October

🅿 🍽 Ⓢ ♿/Lim acc

48 Whithorn Priory and Museum
NX 444403 83 HS
*On A746 in Whithorn, Dumfries &
Galloway*
The site of a 5th-century Christian community of St Ninian, and ruins of a 12th-century Premonstratensian priory.

Mary visited here in 1563. A fine collection of early Christian sculpture is housed in a nearby museum. Visitor centre.

☎ 01988 500508—Open all year; Museum open Easter to October

🅿 Nearby ♿

Other Places to Visit

49 Bolton Castle
*Off A864, 6 miles W of Leyburn,
Yorkshire*
A large and well-preserved medieval castle, built by the Scrope family, the building consists of four massive towers, with joining ranges, constructed around a courtyard.

Mary was imprisoned here from 1568.

☎ 01969 623981—March to October

🅿 🍽 Ⓢ ♿ ♿

50 Carlisle Castle
NY 397563 85 EH
*N of Carlisle town centre,
Cumbria*
Involved often in the centuries of warfare between England and Scotland, Carlisle Castle is a large, impressive and complex medieval castle. David I died here in 1153.

Mary was imprisoned here after fleeing to England in 1568.

☎ 01228 591922—Open all year except Christmas and New Year

🅿 Nearby Ⓢ ♿ ♿

51 Etal Castle
NT 925394 74 EH
*In Etal, 11 miles SW of Berwick
upon Tweed*
It was here that James IV dallied with the lady of the house before going to his death at the disastrous Battle of Flodden in 1513 with many thousand of his men, nobles and churchmen. An

exhibition tells the story of the battle.
Castle open all year; exhibition
only open summer, audio-tape
accompanies tour.

52 Louvre Palace
Paris

The huge and magnificent palace of
the French kings, later enlarged and
used by Napoleon. The palace houses
a huge collection of art, and is entered
from beneath the courtyard by a
unique glass pyramid.

It was in the old part of the palace
that Mary was betrothed to François in
1558.

Open all year

P **S** **WC** F **&** Access

53 Notre Dame Cathedral
Paris

Built on an island in the Seine, Notre
Dame is a large and magnificent
cathedral, which dates from medieval
times.

Mary and François were married here
in 1558.

Open all year except during services.

P Nearby

Index